THE CHRISTIAN IDEA OF GOD

In this book, eminent theologian Keith Ward takes a fresh look at the ancient philosophy of idealism, connects it with findings in modern science, and shows that a combination of good science, good philosophy, and a passion for truth and goodness can underpin religious faith. Going back to first principles, he argues for the idealist view that all knowledge begins with experience. Critically examining the idealism of Plato, Kant, and Hegel, Ward shows how this philosophy is strengthened by knowledge of modern physics and how it can lead to a new and vivid presentation of Christian faith. A work of philosophical rigour that makes clear the rational nature of belief in God, this book challenges the easy assumptions of materialism and the relativity of truth that undermine both science and religion. Ward writes in an accessible and readable style that gives new life and practical usefulness to idealist philosophy.

KEITH WARD is Professor of the Philosophy of Religion at the University of Roehampton. He was formerly Professor of the Philosophy of Religion, University of London, and Regius Professor of Divinity at Oxford. He is the author of many books on religion, philosophy, and theology – including on Kant, comparative theology, and, recently, *Christ and the Cosmos: A Reformulation of Trinitarian Doctrine*, 2015, Cambridge University Press. He is a Fellow of the British Academy and a Canon of Christ Church, Oxford.

D1592864

Cambridge Studies in Religion, Philosophy, and Society

Series Editors

Paul Moser, *Loyola University Chicago*
Chad Meister, *Bethel College*

This is a series of interdisciplinary texts devoted to major-level courses in religion, philosophy, and related fields. It includes original, current, and wide-spanning contributions by leading scholars from various disciplines that (a) focus on the central academic topics in religion and philosophy, (b) are seminal and up to date regarding recent developments in scholarship on the various key topics, and (c) incorporate, with needed precision and depth, the major differing perspectives and backgrounds – the central voices on the major religions and the religious, philosophical, and sociological viewpoints that cover the intellectual landscape today. Cambridge Studies in Religion, Philosophy, and Society is a direct response to this recent and widespread interest and need.

Recent Books in the Series

Roger Trigg
Religious Diversity: Philosophical and Political Dimensions

John Cottingham
Philosophy of Religion: Towards a More Humane Approach

William J. Wainwright
Reason, Revelation, and Devotion: Inference and Argument in Religion

Gordon Graham
Philosophy, Art, and Religion: Understanding Faith and Creativity

THE CHRISTIAN IDEA
OF GOD

A Philosophical Foundation for Faith

KEITH WARD

University of Roehampton and Christ Church, Oxford

CAMBRIDGE
UNIVERSITY PRESS

B
823
.W27
2017

CAMBRIDGE
UNIVERSITY PRESS

University Printing House, Cambridge CB2 8BS, United Kingdom

One Liberty Plaza, 20th Floor, New York, NY 10006, USA

477 Williamstown Road, Port Melbourne, VIC 3207, Australia

4843/24, 2nd Floor, Ansari Road, Daryaganj, Delhi – 110002, India

79 Anson Road, #06–04/06, Singapore 079906

Cambridge University Press is part of the University of Cambridge.

It furthers the University's mission by disseminating knowledge in the pursuit of education, learning, and research at the highest international levels of excellence.

www.cambridge.org
Information on this title: www.cambridge.org/9781108419215
DOI: 10.1017/9781108297431

© Keith Ward 2017

This publication is in copyright. Subject to statutory exception and to the provisions of relevant collective licensing agreements, no reproduction of any part may take place without the written permission of Cambridge University Press.

First published 2017

Printed in the United States of America by Sheridan Books, Inc.

A catalogue record for this publication is available from the British Library.

ISBN 978-1-108-41921-5 Hardback
ISBN 978-1-108-41021-2 Paperback

Cambridge University Press has no responsibility for the persistence or accuracy of URLs for external or third-party internet websites referred to in this publication and does not guarantee that any content on such websites is, or will remain, accurate or appropriate.

Contents

Introduction

There is more than one Christian idea of God, though all share much in common. In this book I aim to set out one main Christian idea which is founded on a philosophical view known as personal idealism.

Idealism in philosophy has nothing to do with being idealistic, which the *Oxford English Dictionary* defines as pursuing usually impractical ideals. Philosophical idealism is the opposite of philosophical materialism, which claims that everything that exists is a form of matter. Idealism holds that matter cannot exist without mind and depends on mind for its existence. Personal idealism holds that there is one supreme mind on which everything else depends and that is personal – that knows, thinks, feels, and intends.

This book tried to defend personal idealism as a philosophy and to show that it is a strong philosophical foundation for Christian belief. The book is thus a work of Christian theology, holding that Christianity has a strong philosophical basis and that Christianity needs such a basis. It is also a work of philosophy, arguing, perhaps unfashionably, that good philosophical argument lends itself naturally to belief in God. Or if that is too strong for modern tastes, it argues that at least Christianity is not just a matter of pure faith, but is closely related to reasonable, plausible, and defensible philosophical theses. The book is written from an explicitly Christian perspective, though its main arguments could easily be transferred – obviously with some adjustments – to other theistic views. I hope that the philosophical arguments will stand up to rigorous inspection on their own and that those interested in philosophy and in religion, whatever exact form their interest takes, will find in this book something worth taking into consideration.

Of course philosophical arguments are always contestable, and it may be felt that this book is too short to deal adequately with all the arguments upon which it depends. That is true. But philosophy has become a very technical discipline, and to deal adequately with any one philosophical thesis that I uphold would need at least one large volume littered with rigorous formal logic. To deal adequately with all the theses I defend would take a whole library. I wished to write a book that was not too long and that was readable and accessible, while dealing with topics that are both philosophically profound and practically important. I do think rigorous argument is important, and I have presented arguments for each thesis I hold and have not shrunk from confronting major problems. But it is impossible to deal with all critical objections or to survey all the vast literature available. I have provided notes pointing to fuller discussions of this sort that can be found elsewhere.

If read in conjunction with *Morality, Autonomy, and God* (Oneworld Press, 2013) and *Christ and the Cosmos* (Cambridge University Press, 2016), the book can be seen as part of a systematic Christian philosophical theology. But this book is meant to stand alone as a cumulative argument giving a philosophical foundation for Christian faith.

I have used – particularly in Chapters 8, 15, 16, and 18 - some material adapted from articles I have published in edited books. Those articles are 'God as the Ultimate Informational Principle' in

Information and the Nature of Reality, edited by Paul Davies and Niels Henrik Gregersen (Cambridge University Press, 2010); 'Cosmos and Kenosis' in *The Work of Love*, edited by John Polkinghorne (SPCK, 2001); and 'Idealism and the Moral Life' in *Idealism and Christian Philosophy*, edited by Steven Cowan and James Spiegel (Bloomsbury, 2016). I am grateful to the publishers for permission to use this material.

PART I

The Nature of Mind

CHAPTER I

What Personal Idealism Is

To be a Christian is to believe that the human person of Jesus of Nazareth is the revelation, in and through a human person, of the nature of God as self-giving love. Jesus is believed to be the vehicle of God's action to liberate humans from the power of greed, hatred, and ignorance and unite them in love with God forever. Jesus is the incarnation – the embodiment – of God in human form and the saviour of the world from sin.

This is a very simple faith, in that all it requires is devotion to Jesus as the human expression of God's love and trust that, through Jesus, God will bring humans into an unbreakable fellowship with the divine life. Millions of people throughout the world require no more than a love of Jesus and a trust in God as their saviour from evil in order to live a full and often heroic Christian life.

Yet the Christian faith is also an intellectually profound vision of human nature and destiny. It is by no means a leap from reason to some sort of wish-fulfilling fantasy. The Gospel of John begins by saying that the creation of the universe was brought about through the Word (*Logos*, the Reason or Wisdom) of God (John 1, 1), and Christians have always insisted that the wisdom of God really is wisdom, not arbitrary whim. God is love, but God is also wisdom, and if philosophy is the love of wisdom, then philosophy should be a form of devotion to divine wisdom.

It cannot be said that all modern philosophers see philosophy that way. For many of them, philosophy is indeed the pursuit of wisdom, but what wisdom shows them, they think, is the weakness of the human mind and its inability to resolve deep questions about human life and destiny. So many modern philosophers do not think that there is a creator God of love and wisdom, and therefore they are bound to see Jesus as a deluded prophet, not the supreme human form of divine love.

Obviously, then, not all philosophical thought is devotion to divine wisdom. Nevertheless, it should not be forgotten that many of the greatest philosophers have seen philosophy as an enquiry into the nature and purpose of the intelligible mind which underlies the physical universe. Plato and Aristotle, Aquinas, Descartes, Leibniz and Spinoza, Locke and Berkeley, Kant and Hegel all saw philosophy in this way. Their views were of course not identical, but they all thought that the most acute human enquiry would show that the heart of reality lay in something akin to intelligence and intellectual beauty – something hard to define and describe, but hard only because it was greater than, not less than, the human mind and the limits of human language.

Not all these philosophers have been Christians, but Christianity is clearly a major philosophical attempt to state the ultimate nature of reality and of human life. Christians therefore, whether they know it or not, are standing in a great tradition of philosophical reflection which can reasonably claim to bear comparison with the most profound philosophies in human history. I want to explore a tradition of Christian philosophy – one that has ancient roots but came into prominence in Europe, particularly in Germany and Britain, in the early nineteenth century. It is the tradition sometimes known as personal idealism: an analysis of the idea of the God of Christianity – a God who creates the physical universe, who is incarnate in a particular human being, and who saves humans from evil and gives them a share in the divine life. As a philosophy, Christianity tries to show that this idea of God is rationally coherent, that it is consistent with the best modern scientific and moral beliefs, and that it gives a strong intellectual foundation to the simple faith of devotion to and trust in Jesus that all Christians share. I do not pretend that this is the only Christian philosophy. I am content to claim that it is a proper and profound philosophy (not an irrational leap of faith) and that it is properly Christian.

Idealism in general is a philosophical position that holds that mind is the only primordial reality and that the whole material universe is a product of mind. The material universe would not exist at all without mind, and the true nature of the universe is that it is an expression or appearance of a basically mental reality. Believers in God should have no difficulty with this, but not all Christians would call themselves idealists.

One reason for this is that some people think idealists deny the existence of a material world altogether. Bishop Berkeley, the best-known eighteenth-century idealist, calls his own view 'immaterialist'[1] and gives the impression that the whole material world is constructed by human minds or that sense impressions are put directly into human minds by God, without the mediation of an external material world. Most idealists, however – like Hegel – do not hold this sort of extreme idealism. They believe that there is a material universe but that it could not exist without one supreme, primordial mind. Human minds may be emergent parts of the material universe, and they may be essentially material and social beings, but the universe of which

[1] See George Berkeley, *Three Dialogues between Hylas and Philonous* (1713), dialogue 3. This certainly gives the impression that God inserts 'ideas' directly into finite minds. But earlier in the third dialogue he speaks of 'creation' as God making the ideas of the universe in the divine mind such as to be perceivable by finite minds. This allows a place for the universe existing in the divine mind in such a way as to be perceivable by finite minds even when not actually perceived by them.

they are part is wholly dependent upon the one supreme mind or Spirit for their existence.

What is the difference of personal idealism, then, from theism, which seems to say exactly that? The fact is that many apparently quite different world views are only really different in their extreme forms. The boundaries between them are rather fuzzy, and at the edges they merge or overlap.

Mind-matter dualism, for instance, in its extreme form, holds that mind and matter are quite different sorts of things or 'substances', each of them existing independently and only coming into contact in accidental or not very positive ways. Thus Plato held that souls were imprisoned in matter but would be better off if they escaped from matter altogether and lived in a disembodied state. More moderate forms of dualism, however, might acknowledge a difference between mind and matter, and yet hold that in humans the two are essentially connected. Moreover, they may insist that matter is essentially dependent upon the one supreme mind of God. This seems to have been Descartes' view, despite the fact that he is often referred to as the founder of dualism.

A world view that appears very different, extreme philosophical monism, holds that mind and matter are two aspects of the same unitary reality and that those aspects are inseparable, so that minds cannot exist without matter (without brains). The philosopher John Searle seems to hold such a view of 'double-aspect monism', and he thinks that the material aspect is the primary causal component in this monistic unity.[2] Less-extreme double-aspect monists, however, may think that the mental aspect also has an important causal role and that each aspect could exist without the other. It is open to such moderate monists to assert the existence of a God (a mind with no

[2] Cf. John Searle, 'The Rediscovery of the Mind', 1992. Searle argues for the irreducible existence of consciousness but maintains that it is caused by and dependent upon the physical brain.

material aspect), and even of a disembodied existence of humans after death.

Idealism, dualism, monism, and theism thus all, in their moderate forms, agree that the whole material universe may depend upon one supreme mind. Why, then, should I wish to defend idealism in particular?

As I shall go on to show, idealism does not see God as a person 'outside' the universe, only occasionally interfering in it, and it does not see God as a changeless 'Pure Form' which the universe cannot affect in any way – both of them fairly common versions of theism. It sees the universe as the progressive and developing self-expression of God (the supreme mind or Self), and God as being changed by the inclusion of created things in the divine being, either now or in the future. God and the material universe thus form a unity, though one in which the mental or spiritual aspect has ontological and causal priority. That is the sort of view I hold. Such an idealism is 'personal' insofar as it holds that the supreme Self has the personal characteristics of knowing, feeling, and willing, even though this being may be much greater than anything we would ordinarily call a 'person'.

Idealism was, at the beginning of the twentieth century, the dominant philosophy in the United Kingdom. Berkeley, Hume, and the other earlier classical British empiricists were also idealists, though they interpreted idealism in very different ways. In India, forms of idealist philosophy have always been present. Sankara and Ramanuja are idealists, and so are many other Indian philosophers who think that the ultimate reality is Brahman, which we can think of as a reality of intelligence and bliss, not just lumps of unconscious matter. Most Buddhists, too, are idealists insofar as they think that reality consists of various conscious states – like perceptions, feelings, and thoughts – and not of material particles. Even though the Buddhist ultimate state of liberation, nirvana, is often said to be beyond description, it is also often spoken of as a state of knowledge and bliss, which implies that it is mind-like in some sense.

There are not so many idealists in modern analytical philosophy, though there are some. And strange as it may seem, some quantum and mathematical physicists are idealists also, thinking that the apparently common-sense world we perceive by means of the senses is not ultimately real and that something like observation (consciousness) is necessary to the very existence of lumps of matter.[3]

So idealism is very much a live option in the world of philosophy, even though it is not very fashionable at present in Europe and North America. There are many varieties of idealism. Some (many Buddhists and some British empiricists) think that there are mental entities (like thoughts and perceptions) which are not reducible to physical entities but that there are no such things as continuing minds (mental substances) which have those properties. Others think that there are minds, but no God or Supreme Mind, on which the universe depends. Still others think that there is an all-including Absolute Reality which is mind-like or intelligent but that it is not properly described as a personal God. And some think that there is one supreme personal mind – that is, the ultimate reality is God.

I belong in this last group, whose members may reasonably be called personal idealists,[4] and I try to explain why I think this is a

---

[3] Cf. the sustained argument in *The Non-Local Universe*, Robert Nadeau and Menas Kafatos (Oxford University Press, 1999), esp. ch. 10. I am delighted that Menas inscribed my copy of this book with the words 'with my best regards for our common view' – just to confirm that there is convergence between idealism and at least some positions of quantum physicists.

[4] There are various forms of personal idealism, but there are two main schools, commonly known as the Californian and the Bostonian. My view is not identical with either but is nearer to the Boston school of Borden Parker Bowne. The California school of George Holmes Howison rejects the idea of one supreme personal creator God.

very reasonable sort of idealism. For personal idealists, the philosophy of idealism is closely connected with the practices of religion, because if there is a God, it makes sense to try to relate consciously to God if possible, or to be prepared to find disclosures of God's nature and purpose in the created universe. It is particularly closely connected with Christianity, because Christianity speaks of a supreme personal God who relates in love to finite creatures.

Idealists do not, in general, attempt to prove the existence of God. That is, after all, a rather odd enterprise, which supposes that the material world is obviously real, whereas God is some sort of unknown entity whose existence we have to prove by some process of inference. Idealism is an attempt to offer a rational interpretation of human experience. The concept of 'God' emerges as a general concept of a mind-like reality which is meant to integrate various sorts of human experience, and it succeeds to the extent that it provides such an integrating interpretation of experience and proves conducive to living a good and fulfilling human life.

God is not an inference from what we know to be real. God is the implicit reality which we know in all our knowing. The philosophical task is to spell out what it means to say that mind is the basis of reality.

Philosophers, almost as a matter of honour, disagree among themselves. So it is no use pretending that personal idealism is seen by philosophers as obviously true. Philosophical reflection on the nature of reality can lead to a number of different conclusions. Partly, this is because of the different interests and starting points that philosophers have. Those who are impressed by the success of the natural sciences, and think that in principle scientific methods can answer every sensible question, feel the attraction of materialism. Those who prefer a more common-sense approach may feel that ordinary language is in order as it is and that there is no need to seek a special, totalising view of 'the nature of reality'. Then there are those who feel that all knowledge begins with experience but that experience does not license any intellectual theories of 'underlying substances' or 'selves', and they incline towards a rigorous sort of minimalist empiricism. Some, however, like me, think that there are important experiences of transcendence and value, and they tend to be attracted by idealism or theism.

None of these philosophical views are clearly more rational than the others, and none of them are matters of 'blind faith'. One thing that philosophy can teach is that reality is ambiguous and its nature is difficult to discern. Humans are just basically diverse, and the best they can do is make their beliefs as coherent and well informed as they can. Thus the first lesson of philosophical reflection is that absolute theoretical certainty is not achievable; that those who are wisest are those who, as Socrates said, know that they know little; and that there is no such thing as the one totally rational view that all intelligent people are bound to accept. Life is more complex than that, and in the end we may all find ourselves having to commit to some beliefs in practice without making claims to final theoretical certainty. That is not irrational. On the contrary, it is supremely rational to see the limits of human intellect and to accept that practical commitment without theoretical certainty is a human necessity.[5] This is especially so if such commitment involves a response to the perception of something that is both morally demanding and personally fulfilling.

Christians may say that their faith is not founded on speculative philosophy but on a passionate response to the experience of encountering a morally demanding and personally fulfilling God

---

[5] Cf. Søren Kierkegaard, *Concluding Unscientific Postscript*, sec. 2, ch. 2, writes of 'an objective uncertainty, held fast through appropriation with the most passionate inwardness'. If the 'uncertainty' is also of immense moral or human importance, it is indeed worthy of such passionate commitment.

in the person of Jesus. That may well be so, but it is important to see that Christian faith is no more a 'leap beyond reason' than any other matter of great importance in human life – like marrying a loved one, choosing a job, or making a serious moral commitment. What personal idealism can do is show the deep reasonableness of Christian faith and help provide answers to some of the problems about faith that Christians may meet as they go through life.

CHAPTER 2

Beginning from Experience

Some people think that material things are the only real things. Rocks, trees, planets, molecules, atoms, and subatomic particles – all these things are real. They exist, and in the end they are the only things that exist. Everything is made up of little chunks of matter, so matter is all that exists.

Minds, we might think, are just complicated arrangements of atoms in the brain. We know that computers are just made of matter, and they seem to 'think' and to 'know things'. So maybe we are just complicated computers. All our thoughts and feelings and sensations are just by-products of the interactions of small bits of matter (neurons) in our brains.[1] Matter is real, but consciousness, thoughts, and feelings are not real. Or even if they are real, they are just complicated clumps of matter. Matter is the basis of reality.

But there are good reasons to doubt this view of reality. One is that it is very difficult to say what 'matter' is. Scientists used to think that all material things were made up of indivisible atoms that had a specific location in space and time; had mass, weight, or gravitational attraction; and moved around with a specific velocity. But since the beginning of the twentieth century that view has been completely overturned.

[1] Francis Crick, in *The Astonishing Hypothesis* (Simon and Schuster, 1994), says, 'You are in fact no more than the behaviour of a vast assembly of nerve-cells and their associated molecules.' People who believe this are called eliminative materialists. There are not many of them (perhaps they are eliminating themselves).

Within the atom there is a whole world of subatomic particles, and it seems that these are not really particles at all. They are more like fields of force, and Heisenberg's Principle of Indeterminacy asserts that particles, like electrons, do not have a specific location and momentum at the same time. They seem to be spread out and only to take on a specific location or velocity when they are subjected to experimental interference. Moreover, in virtually all theories in quantum physics, particles interact with each other non-locally, without immediate spatial contact. In relativity theory, space-time itself bends and contracts, and though space-time does not seem to be material, it is envisaged as a reality which governs the motions of material objects.

Hard lumps of matter seem to have disappeared and have been replaced in science by such strange entities as dark energy, dark matter, superposed particles, and multiple space-times. There are probably forms of causality that we do not yet understand, as well as forces and fields that we have not yet imagined. In the present state of physics, it is hard to put any limit on the forms of existence and interaction that might take place even in our physical universe. In this state of affairs, saying, 'Everything is made of matter' is pretty vacuous, when we cannot state with any precision or exhaustively what the properties of matter are.[2]

It certainly seems impossible to say, 'Everything that exists must exist in our space-time', since some physicists almost routinely speak of other space-times, which probably have fundamental laws and states completely unknown to us. So with what confidence may we say that everything that exists must exist in some space-time or

[2] For a powerful statement of this view, see Paul Davies and John Gribbin, *The Matter Myth* (Penguin, 1992). Ch. 1 is titled 'The Death of Materialism'.

other? This appears to be an unjustifiably restrictive dogma, and such an assertion suggests lack of imagination rather than confirmed scientific theory.

The challenge may be, however, to ask if we have any idea of anything that exists but is not in space-time. That is a challenge which a great many philosophers, and perhaps most notably the eighteenth-century British empiricists, have answered – in my view, definitively. Each human person, they say, is immediately and certainly aware of innumerable things that are not in space-time. These are conscious experiences, often but not always delivered by the senses. The empiricists called them 'Ideas'; later empiricists have called some of them 'sense-data' or 'qualia'. They are immediately apprehended data of consciousness.[3]

The key empiricist move is to say that all knowledge begins with personal experience. Extreme empiricists add that all knowledge is confined to experience. It is important to note, however, that this might well rule out much modern scientific knowledge, which speaks of entities or forces that we cannot directly experience. And, like materialism, extreme empiricism is a rather dogmatically restrictive view.

The more moderate empiricist move strikes me as the right way to start in philosophical enquiries into the nature of reality. Scientifically minded thinkers often profess to find the existence of consciousness a very hard problem, largely because they cannot see how or why conscious experiences arise from the material

---

[3] Probably the best-known defender of this view in modern philosophy is A. J. Ayer, whose 1936 book *Language, Truth, and Logic* based all human knowledge on the existence of sense-data. Some philosophers, like Gilbert Ryle, my own tutor, have denied that sense-data exist. But recent philosophers like Frank Jackson ('What Mary Didn't Know', *Journal of Philosophy* 83, no. 5, 1986) have argued that seeing red for the first time, for example, gives new knowledge. And Thomas Nagel ('What Is It Like to Be a Bat?' *Philosophical Review* 83, no. 4, 1974) defends the view that such phenomenal knowledge is essentially private, not fully conceptually expressible or linguistically communicable to others. That is a view I accept.

structure of the brain. For an empiricist, consciousness is not a problem. It is where enquiry starts and the basis of all our knowledge. It is more of an immediately known fact than is the postulated public space-time of common sense or the almost unpicturable, bendy space-time of relativity physics.

If we ask, 'What do I know immediately, without inference or reference to any complex theory?' then the most obvious candidates are sense-perceptions – sights, sounds, touches, smells, tastes, and bodily sensations. Modern studies of the brain demonstrate that our perceptions of colour and size, for instance, are subjective in the sense that they do not give us knowledge of what exists when it is not being perceived by us. For instance, it is usually said by neuroscientists that it is the brain that constructs coloured images from electrochemical impulses transmitted from our eyes, as they react to stimuli from electromagnetic wavelengths of a limited range of bandwidths. In other words, without the eyes and brain, colour would not exist in the way we see it. There would only be electromagnetic waves. These are perceived as colours, and colours would not exist without a perceiving brain.

That is the story neuroscientists often tell. But an empiricist philosopher will point out that to say the brain constructs perceptions is not an immediate datum of consciousness (as perceived colours are). It is a theory, incorporating facts about the brain that were unknown to generations of humans. Aristotle, for instance, did not believe that the brain was the organ of thought. We now know that if the brain is stimulated in a specific way, various colours will be perceived by the person whose brain it is. So a causal theory is set up connecting the activity of the brain with the perception of colour. This is a good causal theory, confirmed in innumerable cases. But it is still a causal theory. As such, it is subject to experimental confirmation or refutation.

It is logically possible that a person could perceive the colour red when the brain is being stimulated to see what most people would call green, or even when the brain is not active at all. It is also possible that the brain could be stimulated in the correct way but that the person does not see any colour at all. These things are possible (they are not self-contradictory and do not seem to pre-suppose any hidden contradictions), though as far as we know they do not occur.

This is rather like saying that some object may not obey the law of gravity; yet all objects we have ever measured do obey it, and so we make the hypothesis that all objects do. It is a well-confirmed scientific generalisation. Similarly, it is a well-confirmed scientific generalisation that colours are always perceived when, and only when, identifiable brain activity occurs.

As a matter of fact, colour perception can even occur when there are no eyes, if the brain is directly stimulated in the right area. So it is with sounds, smells, and feels. Stimulation of the brain produces them, and the failure of the brain system eliminates them. Of course none of this could possibly show that perceptions do not exist. And at this point the empiricist can point out that we know that brains exist only because we perceive them. But do our perceptions of brains correspond to some objectively, externally existing reality which is exactly like what we perceive?

The common-sense assumption is that of course they do. But then the common-sense assumption about vision is that of course the colours we see really exist in the objective world, when we know that they do not! Something exists – something that produces a coherent, intelligible, regular, predictable set of perceptions. We have a built-in tendency to think that perceptions do not just happen by accident or at random. They must be caused by some-thing other than us. And that something turns out to be remarkably law-like and mathematically elegant. But it is not in itself what we perceive it to be.

It is often not realised how very strange it is that the reality underlying our perceptions is as law-like and predictable as it is. Why should it be true that the law of gravity, as well as the properties of nuclear particles, should be so invariant, so universally applicable, and so mathematically elegant? We could just say that it is a fact, and that is that. But it seems to be a very strange fact that there should be universal laws of nature that give rise to coherent sets of perceptions in many different minds. It is not something we could take for granted, and yet science has no hesitation in assuming that it is true. This is indeed a dogma, a postulate that might well not have been true, that seems to be confirmed by all our (rather limited) experiences but that it is impossible to confirm conclusively (in a possibly infinite universe, there might be exceptions we have not come across).[4]

This may lead us to think that, while the correlation of brain states and perceptions may be universal in our universe, it is not at all bound to be the case. There may be other worlds in which there is no such correlation – though if there were not, beings might not be able to make such good sense of their experiences. Perhaps there could not be any intelligent physical beings at all in such a possible universe, because the highly complex, integrated, and relatively stable physical substratum on which brain-perception correlations could be based would never come into existence.

Such thought experiments emphasise that brain-perception correlations are contingent. They do not have to exist, and they need not be the way they are. But these thought experiments also suggest

[4] In a well-known paper, 'The Unreasonable Effectiveness of Mathematics in Natural Sciences' (*Communications in Pure and Applied Mathematics* 13, no. 1, 1960), Eugene Wigner writes of the almost miraculous gift we have: that mathematics fits objective reality so perfectly yet shows reality to be very unlike our common-sense perception of the world.

that if brain-perception correlations did not exist as they do, physically embodied intelligent minds like ours could not exist at all.

The brain does exist in objective reality, but in that reality it does not look like three pounds of jelly all crumpled up into a squishy grey mess. That is what a brain looks like to us. In the world that we perceive, we can poke the brain, cut bits off it, and stick electrodes into it. The perceived world is real. It exists. But it is not the world as it really is. It is not what the philosopher Immanuel Kant called the world of 'things-in-themselves'.

Kant – who called himself a 'transcendental' or 'critical' idealist – distinguished in the 'Critique of Pure Reason' (1781) the world of phenomena, or appearances to the senses, from the world of noumena, or things as they exist in themselves. Phenomena are largely constructed by the mind, with its categories and forms of thought. Noumenal reality is theoretically unknowable but is certainly very unlike the phenomenal world. In modern physics, Niels Bohr largely followed this Kantian division between an intelligible reality and the perceived world, and physicists like Bernard D'Espagnat, the French quantum physicist, speak of the quantum world as a 'veiled reality' very unlike the world of solid-coloured, three-dimensional objects that we perceive by means of the senses.[5]

So what we now have is this: our manipulation of part of the world-as-perceived-by-us (namely, someone's brain) causes changes to occur in law-like and predictable ways in part of the world-as-perceived-by-someone-else. We only know this is true because they tell us – that is, other people intentionally cause changes in our perceptions which we take to inform us correctly of what is happening to their perceptions.

[5] See Bernard D'Espagnat, *Reality and the Physicist* (Cambridge University Press, 1990).

Now we see the major problem of empiricism: the world of objective, shared reality seems to disappear into lots of subjective, private realities. Sets of perceptions are never really shared by other people. We cannot even confirm that they exist by any direct perceptions of our own. That is why we can never be absolutely sure that ants or bees are conscious. We have to take some of our perceptions as informing us about perceptions we can never have.

That is why perceptions need to be interpreted by thought. To make sense of our experience, we have to assume that there is a public world which is the law-like cause of our perceptions and that there are other sets of perceptions (other minds) which we can never know in the way that we know our own perceptions. These assumptions – of an objective, unperceived world and of the existence of other minds that we can never directly perceive – are basic to human knowledge. Experience may be the starting point of knowledge. But experience needs to be interpreted, and the ideas of objective causality, of other minds, and of the purposive manipulation of parts of our experience (e.g. in communicating our thoughts to others) are basic to such interpretation. Thought constructs an explanatory framework to make sense of personal experiences.

If we consider the statement 'The brain constructs perceptions', we can see that in one sense it is true. Without the brain, and given the causal laws of our universe (which, as I have pointed out, did not have to be the way they are), perceptions as we have them would not exist. But in another sense it can be misleading. It can give the impression that the physical brain does all the causal work and that perceptions and thoughts are a by-product of brain activity which are not really essential to or causally operative in the physical process. But in the empiricist view, perceptions and thoughts are not by-products of physical processes; they are basic and causally operative.

Without thoughts we would not be able to interpret our sub-jective experiences as experiences of an objective world. There would be no knowledge of the nature of the universe. It would not be possible to place a value on anything, to consciously prefer one thing to another, or to seek a goal because it is desired. The idea of a value is the idea that one thing is to be preferred to another, and so it involves knowledge (what are the things one may or may not value?), a sense that some things are worthwhile for their own sakes (as pleasure is to be preferred to pain, for example), and a feeling that one has some capacity to seek out or choose some things in preference to others (a sense of purpose). In a world that was purely physical, there would be no consciousness able to value some things more than others, and if experiences were purely passive, we would not have the sense of being able to choose some things rather than others. Further, it is that sense of choosing a possible future because it is of value that gives rise to the idea of purpose, of acting for the sake of obtaining a future good. Without consciousness there is no value. Without value there is no purpose.

A universe without consciousness would just consist of one thing after another, but it would make no sense to say that one thing was 'better' than another or that there were any goals towards which the universe or anything in it was aiming. Only when consciousness exists can values be appreciated and enjoyed and become goals worth aiming at. If knowledge, value, and choice are real elements of existence, then they are different in kind from and not reducible to physical properties such as position, mass, and electric charge.

There are philosophers today who would disagree with these points and who seek to give an account of value and purpose in purely physicalist terms. The literature on this topic is vast and often highly technical, and to try to deal adequately with it would stop this book in its tracks. What can be reliably said is that the debate is ongoing and unresolved. Philosophers like Colin McGinn think it is unresolvable in principle.[6] I must content myself with saying that I think the empiricists are correct in holding that all knowledge begins with experience. I suggest that experience involves thought as well as perception, and that thoughts are necessary if perceptions are believed to give knowledge of an objective world. Perceptions and thoughts have a distinctive kind of reality which is not reducible to the sort of purely physical properties with which the natural sciences deal. Perceptions have phenomenal qualities (e.g. what it is like to see green or red) which unobserved objects do not have, and thoughts presuppose mental acts which generate, communicate, and order them. Unobserved physical objects do not act, for acting, in its primary sense of doing something to achieve some goal, is a form of causality which operates only by means of knowledge, evaluation, and intention – properties which unobserved physical objects lack. When an agent acts, it does so on the basis of knowing what is possible, evaluating what possible futures are worth pursuing, and intending to pursue some of them.

It is only when we introduce perceptions and thoughts that we can form an idea of value and of purposive agency. Since these are primary data of experience, from which all human knowledge derives, no theory that denies their existence is plausible. Consciousness is not some odd and inexplicable aberration in a basically material world. It is the origin and basis of all human knowledge. In a sense, it is matter that needs explaining, not conscious experiences.

It may well be that some material substratum is needed which can provide data for knowledge and opportunities for choices and

---

[6] This is a position sometimes known as the New Mysterianism and is expounded by Colin McGinn in *The Problem of Consciousness* (1991). As such, it is not a defence of dualism, but rather holds that the human mind is incapable of understanding the nature and causes of consciousness.

actions in a public and shared environment. But for a materialist, it is very hard to account for the existence of consciousness, which has to be an accidental and unforeseen anomaly in the natural world. As far as one can see, and certainly on a materialist account, conscious-ness is not necessary for humans to operate as they do, with all the beliefs about free will that they have. Consciousness would just be a functionless add-on to a world of completely explanatory physical laws. For idealists, however, the existence of consciousness makes a difference and has contributed to the evolutionary efficiency of the human species. It is because humans are conscious that they have been able to plan, evade capture by predators, and learn to hunt animals and plant seeds. Consciousness does seem to have played an important role in enabling proto-humans to survive preferen-tially over competing species. And that suggests that consciousness really does exist as a new factor in the evolutionary story, adding new causal powers to organic beings.[7]

Furthermore, for idealists, who make consciousness primary, it is relatively easy to explain why matter should exist. Matter provides an intelligible environment which can generate objects of consciousness (perceptions) and possibilities for goal-directed action. On such an account, the whole material world can be seen as an instrument for bringing about particular sorts of consciousness and providing them with objects of knowledge and opportunities for purposive action. Far from consciousness being a by-product of matter, the physical universe is a precondition of and a means to the emergence of particular forms of embodied consciousness.

---

[7] This addition of new causal powers and phenomenal properties to basically physical entities is sometimes known as 'emergentism'. A main defender of this view from the perspective of a biologist is Arthur Peacocke, whose book *Paths from Science towards God* (Oneworld Press, 2001) outlines one version of emergentism. Another version can be found in my *More than Matter* (Lion Hudson, 2010), where I call it 'dual-aspect idealism', in order to distinguish it from John Searle's dual-aspect materialism.

For empiricists, the public world – with its shared space-time and continuing physical objects of a largely unpicturable nature – is an inference or postulate which makes sense of the coherence and integrated complexity of perceptions. If you ask the question 'Where in space-time are these perceptions?' it is obvious that the question makes no sense. Publicly shared space-time is an inference generated from perceptions. It is not a perception or part of a perception. Nor are perceptions 'in' it. If we think of visual perception, then we can say something like this: each person has a visual field roughly oval in shape which contains a two-dimensional array of coloured patches, clear in the middle and blurred at the edges. From this array, thought constructs the idea of a public space containing three-dimensional objects, which is shared by other persons. We place our perceptions in public space – we see objects. But the perceptions themselves, as immediately perceived phenomena, are in a private two-dimensional space (three-dimensional if you include time), not shared by others, with a finite and moveable boundary.

The same is true of all our sensory perceptions. There is a finite and private sound-space, touch-space, smell-space, taste-space, and visual-space. All these spaces are coordinated by thought to generate the idea of a single, possibly infinite and public space of objects which generate all these perceptions through the mechanisms of the body and brain.

For an empiricist, then, all our sense-data are not physical objects in space-time. There are many private phenomenal spaces which thought integrates into the abstract idea of one public (and unpicturable) space-time. Thus there are perceptions, which form the basis of knowledge. There are thoughts that do the integrating, and so the mental activity of thinking is presupposed to the very idea of an objective physical world. There are also feelings which evaluate perceptions, seeing some as attractive and pleasurable, and others as ugly or painful. There are memories and intentions for the future. None of these things are locatable in public space-time.

This suggests that you are not just a lot of material particles, with properties like position in space, mass (weight), electric charge, velocity, and so on. In fact, those are not the most important things about you. They are not the things that make you a unique person. What matters most to you is your total experience, your inner life. Your inner life is totally unique; no one else has an inner life exactly like you do.

It is important to see that this does not deny that you have many material properties and that these are important too. Of course, you have a body and a material brain. But you also have a total experience of perceptions, thoughts, and feelings, and that 'inner life' is what makes you totally unique.

CHAPTER 3

The Unitary Self

When you say that minds are real, you mean that there are lots of sets of total experiences just like yours – there are many minds. They really do exist, and are not just illusions. But of course minds do not just exist for one moment of time. You do not exist as a succession of separate experiences, each existing only for a moment without any inner connection to each other. Some total experiences (a totality consisting of many different sensory and feeling states integrated so as to form one experience) are connected to others so that they form a continuing stream of experiences, related to each other in a special way.[1] Since there are many minds in existence, there are many different streams of experiences, but they are not connected to other streams so as to form one continuing super-experience.

For instance, part of my experience now is a feeling of pain in my leg. I will continue to feel that pain for at least five minutes, and after that I will remember that I had the pain, and that it has now ceased. The pain continues to be part of my experience for many moments, and then the memory of it continues in my experience for

---

[1] A good exposition of this point can be found in Peter Strawson's book *Individuals* (Methuen, 1959), which develops the idea of persons as streams of experience. Strawson argues that such streams are 'possessed' by a subject-agent which must be embodied if it is to be publicly identifiable, though it could logically be disembodied as a 'past-person'. He does not explore the possibility that there could be different forms of embodiment for the same experience-stream, a possibility that, as I shall argue, is essential to the Christian idea of the 'resurrection of the body'.

quite a long time. This is an 'inner connection' between experiences. Each of us can anticipate having a pain in future, can fear the future pain, can experience it, and can then remember having had it. That pain, the fear of it, the experience of it, and the memory of it all belong to just one stream of experiences. Nobody else (no other stream of experiences) can feel fear that I am going to suffer pain in the same way that I can or can remember having had my pain. Streams of experience do not overlap. Each stream is a unique series of internally connected total experiences. I (this stream of experiences) cannot have your pains!

So 'you' and 'I' do not just exist for a moment and then cease to exist. Music is a good example of this truth. When we hear the last note of a piece of music, is that a completely new experience? Or does the way we hear it depend on all the notes that have gone before? When we hear the last note of a tune, we hear it not just as a new experience but rather as the end of a tune. That means that we must have heard a series of notes as one tune, not just as a series of quite separate notes. In other words, our experience extends over time, and (until memory fails) it is cumulative and developing. It increases in knowledge and understanding over time. The same person hears the beginning and the middle and the end of a tune, and hears the whole thing – not as a series of notes, but as one tune. The tune as a whole is part of one experience, part of one mind. So minds endure through time, each mind following a separate track which is quite unique.

Minds are not just successions of passive experiences. When we look into our minds to observe the various experiences that are taking place, we focus attention on our own minds. That focussing is an act, even though it may not involve any bodily movement. It is a mental act. So part of our experience is the experience of acting, of contemplating, thinking, and understanding.

This means that we are not just passive observers of experiences. We are not just streams of experiences. We are agents who can, at least to some extent, influence and shape the sorts of experiences we have. We interpret our experiences so that they have meaning: they provide knowledge of an external reality, and they connect the items of our experience to form a narrative history, with its own dominant values and aims.

So, when I become aware of the feelings and thoughts I have, I am able to reflect on what my real values should be, what sorts of things I should really be aiming at. And I can begin to aim at those things, with a conscious directing of effort.

It is possible to distinguish four main stages in such reflection. First, there is bringing to awareness the feelings, thoughts, and desires that we have. This is understanding. Second, there is deciding what mental states we think are worth aiming at and possible for us. This is evaluation. Third, there is setting about to obtain those states and to set aside tendencies which make it hard for us to obtain them. This is intention. And fourth, there is the enjoyment of the states when we achieve them. This is affective knowledge.

All these things – self-knowledge, evaluation of what is good, the choice of goals to aim at, and the fully focussed enjoyment of those goals – need concentrated and effective action. Minds are agents who can shape their experiences, feelings, and thoughts – not totally but to some degree. To that extent, they are responsible for their inner lives. And they are responsible, too, for shaping the inner lives of others as they constantly interact with other people.

This suggests that what you really are, what makes you the person you are, is not just your genes or your bodily structure. It is the experiences that make up your mind, your inner self. And it is what you make of these experiences, how you react to them, what you do with them. It gives you the basis of shaping your mind so that some experiences are cultivated and others set aside. You become, with luck, more the sort of mind you would really wish to be. It suggests that you are a quite unique person who is capable of being aware of your innermost nature and who also has some ability to shape what you will become in future. It gives you the beginning of self-awareness, self-acceptance, and self-control. And of course it will make you aware that all other persons have the same possibilities and tendencies, so that they must be taken into full account when you make these sorts of decisions.

We are not just passively tossed about by the experiences that happen to us. We have some control over them, and we are responsible for how we respond to them. We can shape the streams of experience that we are. We are partly self-directing streams of experience. We can create our own inner lives – sometimes not very much, it is true, but it is very important to do so when we can.

Some philosophers have denied that there is a continuing agent self. Bertrand Russell complained that Descartes should not have said, 'I think, therefore I am.' He should have said 'I think, therefore there are thoughts.' There is a succession of thoughts, but there does not have to be a thinker.

Similarly, David Hume said, 'For my part, when I enter most intimately into what I call myself, I always stumble on some particular perception or other . . . I never catch myself' (*A Treatise of Human Nature*).[2] But that is hardly surprising. The self is that which perceives, and it is not itself perceived as an observable thing. Perhaps one could think of a perception without a perceiver, but, as Bishop Berkeley was keen to point out, perceptions are passive; they occur but they do not act. Even as I reflect on my perceptions, there

---

[2] David Hume, *A Treatise of Human Nature*, book 1, part 4, sec. 6.

is something present which is not itself a perception – namely the reflection upon them. That reflection can make them sharper or clearer, can let them pass quickly or hold them in attention, can wonder what their nature is. Reflection is an activity, and is known as such. There is an immediately known difference between a percept unattended to and a percept which is held in focus for a span of time. Is that just a difference in the nature of the percept? Well, it is such a difference, but there is something else too. The difference is caused. It is brought about. It does not just happen. What causes it is my focussing attention or not. I may not be the cause of the percept, but I am a cause of how, in what way, it is perceived, and thus of how it exists in my experience. This sense of active attending is as much an element of experience as are percepts themselves. It is a piece of basic knowledge.

It follows that to the perceptions and thoughts which are essential to human experience we must add the idea of a subject which has such perceptions and affective knowledge, and which is also an agent in thinking and intending. Such a subject cannot be purely physical. There is no purely physical subject, for the brain is a collection of physical parts which has no central controlling mechanism (something that Descartes misleadingly sought for in the pineal gland). That which integrates and has introspective knowledge of non-spatial qualia and abstract thoughts will itself be non-spatial.

The idea of a non-spatial subject-self may seem odd. For do humans not act as physical persons in a physical environment? Of course they do. But as neuroscientists are fond of pointing out, there is no quasi-physical 'little man' inside the brain that is acting. Yet the thought that the whole brain – just a collection of physical parts – is acting as one continuous agent seems implausible. It is not surprising that neuroscientists sometimes say that the idea of a subject-self is actually an illusion, an imaginary construction.[3] Philosophers like Daniel Dennett hold that different parts of the brain are responsible for responding to stimuli in different ways and that there is no unitary 'self' at all.[4] This is a form of philosophical schizophrenia for which diverse brain functions may overlap or compete, and the human person disintegrates into a bundle of different physical functions.

No psychiatrist, however, is happy to meet someone who is just a collection of brain functions. Part of Jungian therapy, for instance, aims at integration of the self. There are different and often competing sets of desires and dispositions in the human person, and often people can live with that. But if the condition becomes extreme, then a person is seen as in need of therapy. The achieving of a fully integrated self, in which all dispositions are ordered harmoniously and in fulfilling ways, is (or should be) an ideal of psychiatric medicine. One of life's major tasks is the achievement of a sense of self, of one continuing and rationally ordered life where appropriate goals can be formulated and pursued. The human subject does struggle with mental dispositions that often have physical causes, and while the subject can inform and influence the physical brain to some extent, that brain is frequently an unhelpful constraint on the freedom of the subject. The sense of a unitary self is something to be achieved by

[3] The idea of the self as an illusion is canvassed by the neuroscientist V. S. Ramachandran ('The notion of one unitary self may well be an illusion', *The Tell-Tale Brain* (Windmill, 2012, p. 247) and can also be found in Stephen Hawking's book *The Grand Design* (Bantam, 2011), where he speaks, almost in passing, of the 'illusion' of free will (p. 45), which entails the denial that there is one continuing free agent-self. The problem is, of course, that there is no physical subject to be found. But interestingly, Hawking later, in the same book, holds that consciousness actually determines physical history ('We create history by our observation, rather than history creating us', p. 179). This lacuna between physical determinism and the causal priority of consciousness remains unresolved in the work of some quantum physicists.

[4] Daniel Dennett, in *Consciousness Explained* (Penguin, 1991), calls this a 'multiple drafts' theory. There are different parts of the brain with different stimulus-response functions, and they do not integrate into one whole.

discipline, even under the best conditions, and that is one primary task of the religious life.

Christians are well aware that humans are not as they are meant by the Creator to be. A large part of the ministry of Jesus was dealing with the mental pathologies that were considered to be demon possessions in his time. The healing of the mind can helpfully be seen as the achievement of an integrated and unitary sense of self. One of the things that Christians mean by the 'fall' of humanity is the perception that although we are meant to be unitary selves, we seem doomed to fail to achieve that ideal. The ideal, nonetheless, remains, and a major Christian belief is that the love of God, known in Jesus Christ and placed within human lives by the divine Spirit, can and will ultimately accomplish in us that which we cannot achieve by our own power.

It is not morally, psychologically, or spiritually desirable to accept that one is just a composite and largely fragmented physical entity. Just as different sense perceptions – touch, sight, and sound – are integrated into one experience, so different mental capacities are, to a greater or lesser extent, unified into aspects of one free and responsible subject-self, and such conscious unification is a fulfilment of human personhood, not the cultivation of an illusion. And just as sense perceptions and thoughts are non-spatial entities, so their subject is a non-spatial continuant, though it is strongly integrated with the structure of a brain, body, and social world, which provides the self with its natural and proper environment.[5]

---

[5] This case is argued by John Foster in *The Immaterial Self* (Routledge, 1991), where the 'dualist' idea of a non-physical subject and a physical brain and body is defended. It should be noted that Foster also wrote *The Case for Idealism* (Routledge, 1982). The two books together provide a defence of what I have called 'double-aspect idealism', for which human minds are integrated with a physical environment, but that environment is itself dependent upon the existence of one supreme mind. Richard Swinburne, in *The Evolution of the Soul* (Oxford University Press, 1986), also defends such a dualistic view, though I suspect that he would be less keen on calling it a form of idealism.

CHAPTER 4

The Self as Agent

In Chapter 2 I argued that eliminative materialism simply fails to accept the primary basis of human knowledge in personal experience. It seems quite clear to me that perceptions and thoughts exist and that their existence must be taken into account in any satisfactory philosophy. But it may be thought more difficult to show that the subject-self actually has causal efficacy in the physical world — that it has real, effective, if limited and sometimes frustrated, agency. Could the sense of free causal agency which characterises human thought and action be illusory? Could it simply be a sense produced by the firing of neurons in the brain but not really having any causal effect? I think I know when I am attending closely to some perception and when I am not. That seeming knowledge cannot be denied, but what could be said is that I am deluded. I have the feeling that I am actively attending, but in fact what is happening is that neurons are firing which gives me that feeling. All the causality lies in the physical (and unobserved) neuron firing. My sense of acting is an illusion and is just a feeling produced by the neurons as a by-product.[1]

[1] The best-known example of this is Benjamin Libet's experiment, which is claimed to show that the brain 'decides' to act (initiates a 'readiness potential') before a conscious decision to act is made. Libet himself, however, believed that the subject remained free to inhibit the readiness potential, and so was a believer in free mental causation (see his paper 'Do We Have Free Will?' in *The Volitional Brain*, ed. Libet, Freeman, and Sutherland Imprint Academic, 1999). The conditions of the experiment are so artificial that it is dubious whether its results would apply to real-life situations of decisive and morally important decisions. And it is hard to see how such real-life decisions could be tested under

This is a sophisticated and controversial theory that strongly conflicts with common sense. I think I act, but the theory shows that I am never a real cause, or perhaps that my sense of acting is identical with, and reducible to, neuronal discharges. My brain acts, and I call that action 'mine'. Yet I have already argued that common sense does not provide an accurate account of reality as it is in itself. So could it not be true in this case that common sense is just inaccurate?

In considering this possibility, it is important to distinguish between an 'appearance' and an 'illusion'. If I see a red chair in front of me, this is an appearance to me of something that would not be solid, red, and three-dimensional if it was not being observed by me. But it is not an illusion, as if I were to think it red when it was not red in any respect at all. It really is red as it appears to me, and it is really not red as it is in itself, though this is the real causal basis of its appearance as red to me. However, if the physical determinist theory is true, then if I believe I am free to act, whereas in fact it is my neurons causing me to do so, my belief is not just an appearance; it is an illusion. This is because in believing I am free, I believe that I am not wholly caused to act by my neurons (or by anything else; part of the cause of my action is my free choice of a future state). But on the physical determinist view, that belief would be false. Appearing to be free contradicts being actually determined, whereas appearing to be red to me does not contradict being colourless when not appearing to me.

So on the theory of materialism there is a contradiction between what I naturally believe (that I am free to form beliefs) and what is actually the case. I cannot believe both. Alvin Plantinga has argued that I cannot accept the materialist view as reliably established,

experimental conditions. Perhaps this remains one of McGinn's insoluble problems – in which case mental causation cannot be ruled out by fiat.

because a purely materialist account of consciousness, which denies causal efficacy to conscious thought, is self-refuting.[2] If a complete materialist account can be given of apparently mental activity, and if conscious contents have no causal role, then the generation of apparent and freewheeling mental contents could be anything at all without affecting behavioural outcomes. On a naturalistic evolutionary account, genetically based modifications are preserved if they enable genes to replicate more fruitfully. Freewheeling conscious states could, on that account, have no such function. So there is little reason to think that they give a true or accurate account of how things really are. Indeed, if belief in freedom is an illusion, then this is a case where an inaccurate account of the world has come to be widely accepted. That shows that our beliefs do not give a reliable account of how the world is. Then it follows that my belief that free will is illusory is not reliable either. Even worse, there is little reason to think that any of my beliefs are reliable. Any commitment to truth in science or philosophy becomes suspect.

To avoid this depressing conclusion, I must accept that if rationally justifiable beliefs are possible, determinism must be false. But suppose I am so convinced of materialism that I continue to think that my belief in freedom is an illusion. Then if I am rational, I will have to give up belief in freedom. This may not matter for many things in my life. I can still go on concentrating on a philosophical problem even if I know my mental processes are physically determined (though I may decide that it is not worth the effort). But it may matter a great deal if I have a difficult moral problem or if I wonder whether it is just for God to punish me for sins I was physically caused to commit. If I believe I am not free to do other than my neurons determine me to do, I may decide that

---

Alvin Plantinga, *Where the Conflict Really Lies* (Oxford University Press, 2011), part 4.

making heroic struggles to come to a morally correct conclusion is simply not worth it, and I will just do whatever comes naturally. If I believe that God is unjust to punish me for what I could not help, I may cease to believe in God.

Such decisions would admittedly be paradoxical, for I will be changing my beliefs and actions because of a process of reasoning, whereas the determinist view I am theoretically accepting says that I cannot change anything by just reasoning. I simply falsely believe that I am changing my beliefs for a good reason (in order to achieve a more rational belief). Such teleological causes (changing something in order to achieve some foreseen and desired state) are impossible on the determinist thesis. The final twist of the logical knife is that if I know it is false that I am being more reasonable, then I cannot defend my determinist theory on the ground that it is more reasonable than the alternative. It is like saying, 'I believe for good reasons that it is impossible to believe anything for good reasons.' If this statement is true, it is false. Consequently, it cannot be coherently uttered. This paradox can, of course, be avoided if one accepts that one can come justifiably to believe something as a result of a process of reasoning. In that case, since it is probably true that all human beliefs have causal correlates in brain states, one is accepting that free creative thinking has causal efficacy in the physical world.

This is hardly a surprising conclusion, since all it says is that conscious knowledge and freely chosen responses make a difference to what happens in the world. The only plausible reason to doubt this is a commitment to a 'closed' view of scientific laws which holds that such laws give a complete account of the causal framework so that there is no place for 'free', non-physically determined causality in physical reality. Such a closed view has, however, become very suspect in modern science. There are some main features of contemporary science which strongly suggest that we should see the laws of physical nature as much more 'fuzzy' and open than the closed view holds.[3] We cannot, on grounds of a commitment to natural science, rule out the possibility of free and physically undetermined causes – the actions of personal subject-selves, which actions are determined by envisaged goals selected by the agents themselves out of a range of non-physically determined alternatives.

The closed view of scientific laws is also queried by Heisenberg's Principle of Indeterminacy. That principle states, on the usual interpretation, that subatomic particles cannot have both precise position and momentum at the same time. This already introduces a degree of vagueness and uncertainty into the knowable structure of the natural order. Then again, virtually all quantum theories entail that subatomic particles are entangled, so that they are affected by changes in paired particles (particles which have once interacted) instantaneously over enormous distances. Since in the early universe virtually all particles were entangled with each other, this means that in any situation particles may be affected by things that occur even light years away. This makes it impossible to provide a complete account of all causal factors in any physical situation.

There are other features of modern science that lead to the same conclusion. For instance, the double-slit experiment shows that physical changes occur (wave functions 'collapse') when measurements or observations take place. This means that the physical order cannot be regarded as completely explicable without taking

---

[3] See John Polkinghorne: 'We have no compelling grounds for regarding current theories as being more than a form of approximation to actual physical reality as it is encountered in the limit of effective isolatability', in *Exploring Reality* (Yale University Press, 2005), p. 34. Polkinghorne, once Professor of Mathematical Physics at Cambridge and later an Anglican priest, often reiterates this point, that 'laws of physics' are approximations which only apply perfectly in artificially isolated experimental conditions.

observations and measurements (which are or essentially relate to mental states) into account. In addition, the fairly recent discovery of dark energy and dark matter suggests that there are many sorts of forces as yet unknown to science. Finally, chaos theory, while giving a deterministic account of the evolution of a wave function, entails that tiny microcosmic fluctuations in conditions far from equilibrium can give rise to unpredictable major changes in the macrocosmic world. All these experimentally well-established conclusions show that the physical world is not a closed and complete system, and that many causal influences may be at work which, while not contradicting the physical laws of which we are aware, are not explained by such laws alone.

Rom Harre and Nancy Cartwright, among other philosophers of science, maintain that belief in absolute, unbreakable, and universal laws of nature is not necessary or even consistent with actual scientific practice. The principles of order in nature are much more local, diverse, piecemeal, emergent, and holistic than the old 'Newtonian' (or, better, LaPlacean) model of one set of absolute and universal laws. Perhaps instead of using the model of 'laws', it may be better to speak of the 'powers' and 'capacities' of objects, which may be realised in different local contexts and which are sensitive to novel background conditions that may never have existed before.[4]

To all this one may add that, as David Hume said, the theory that every event is sufficiently determined by some previous event together with some general laws can never be proved, and it is completely mysterious what could cause it to be true in every possible case. In other words, the case from science and philosophy against a causally efficacious freedom of goal-directed action has

[4] See the essays in *Re-Thinking Order*, ed. Nancy Cartwright and Keith Ward (Bloomsbury, 2016), and Nancy Cartwright, *The Dappled World* (Cambridge, 1999).

become rather weak. It certainly seems too weak to undermine our natural belief that in thinking and in acting, humans are not determined, though of course they are influenced and constrained, by purely physical conditions.

A scientifically influenced theory of physical determinism is not strong enough to undermine our ordinary belief in freedom, because such a theory is undermined by recent developments in the understanding of scientific laws and forms of causality. Furthermore, there seems to be a fundamental difference between forms of causal explanations in science and the sorts of explanation that can be given of human action and reasoning. For instance, consideration of whether freedom is real or illusory presupposes that one is able to consider evidence, marshal arguments for and against, and come to a reasoned decision which is truth-claiming. Such a process of reasoning and truth-claiming – aimed at a consciously entertained future state – is very different from the general law-governed nature of physical processes, which blindly follow general principles without thought of the future, of reasonableness, or of truth.

In the case of human actions, persons bring about an event for a reason. They envisage a goal and act in order to achieve it. It is an essential part of a human action that it should be oriented to an envisaged future state. The act of bringing about may produce an effect slightly different from what one has envisaged, but at least the act was aimed at something future and envisaged in some way.

In the case of physical causality, it is generally accepted that physical causes do not act for reason. They bring about effects in accordance with some sort of necessity, some sort of general law, of which no one is conscious and which no one intends. The brain is a physical entity, so if it causes states, it does not do so in order to bring about some future state. But a personal agent does bring about states in order to bring about an envisaged future state. So personal causality is of quite a different nature than physical causality.[5] This means that it is an inadequate account of agency to say that 'the brain caused me to think of this'. Personal causality has to be operative in order to bring about envisaged future states – and that involves intentionality (envisaging objects that do not actually exist), purpose, and value (valuing states one wishes to bring about). These are mental, not physical, factors.

Arguments continue to rage in modern philosophy about whether intentional states can be reduced to physical states. I can safely say that no one has managed such a reduction yet. And I am pretty sure that a reduction is impossible in principle, because they really are different types of causality. One requires general laws, and the other requires conscious states and purposive acts.

The upshot is that there really are irreducibly purposive acts; we are directly aware of them in concentrating, attending, and thinking; and the brain as a physical organ is not the sole and sufficient cause of such acts. An adequate analysis of experience as the basis of all human knowledge should therefore include the experience of purposive action.[6]

Purposive actions, like experiences, are not discrete momentary events. There is a continuity of action over time, sometimes over large stretches of time. If I intend to write a book, that may take years, and the agent who thinks and writes will be the same agent

[5] In *The Big Questions in Science and Religion* (Templeton, 2008) and elsewhere, I distinguish between nomological explanation and axiological explanation. The former is normally used in the natural sciences, where an initial state plus a general mathematically formulable law explain a consequent state. The latter is used in the human sciences and in history and personal affairs, where a state is explained by the conscious envisaging of a future state and an intentional action in order to bring about that state. These two forms of explanation seem to be quite different from each other, and neither can be reduced to the other.

[6] For a defence of causally efficacious ('libertarian') free will, see T. J. Mawson, *Free Will: A Guide for the Perplexed* (Continuum, 2001), and also Richard Swinburne, *Mind, Brain and Free Will* (Oxford University Press, 2013).

throughout the process. I begin the book and I, the same I, complete it. So we have a sense of continuing agency through time, a purposive cause which is not just the brain. Just as there is a unique stream of experiences that form a special sort of unity (the unity of 'my' experience), so there is a unique agency through-out all my experiences which at least to some extent can shape and influence how these experiences occur and how they are integrated into the flow of experience. This is what has traditionally been called a mind, self, or soul.

There is no question that this unity of experience and agency is correlated with the activity of a specific brain. But experience is more than the electrochemical processes of the brain, and action is more than the physically causal activity of brains. Some modern philosophers apparently find it impossible to think of a sort of reality that is not in public physical space and a sort of agency that is not wholly physical. 'Where are experiences?' they may say, as though experiences are impossible if they are not located some-where in space, 'And where is the causal agent?' as though if it is not located in the brain it cannot exist.

Physicists, on the other hand, generally have little problem with imagining that there are objects not in our space-time (they could be in some other universe). Why should it be the case that all objects must be in some public space? That is just a dogma of materialism, and it seems unduly restrictive. Some mathematicians imagine that numbers are objects that exist, but not in space. Plato thought that Forms (*eide*) did not exist in space but were more real than things that did exist in space. Laws of nature and moral truths, if there are such things, do not exist as objects in space. And of course God does not exist in space. Are all these things to be declared impossible, just because they cannot be imagined by materialists? I suggest that non-spatial agents and subjects of streams of experience exist and that they are closely correlated with brains, which provide information about a spatial world of objects and set limits to the sorts of actions that are possible in that world.

It is quite consistent with empiricism to hold that there exist such non-spatial agents and subjects of experience and that they are directly known in experience. Such a form of empiricism is committed to saying that experience gives reliable knowledge of things that exist beyond experience. There are the independently existing objects in the physical world, and there are the non-spatial agents and subjects of experience which have traditionally been called souls in European philosophy.

It is important to see that in the Christian tradition the soul is not some extra bit in addition to the mind. The word 'soul' (*psyche*) has been interchangeable with the word 'mind' since the time of Aristotle, whose work *Peri Psyche* has usually been translated into English as *On the Soul* and into Latin as *De Anima*. For Christians, as for Aristotle, the human mind is seen as essentially embodied, though Aristotle did believe that there was an unembodied mind, the mind of God. If we speak of 'the souls of men and women' in English, we usually mean just 'embodied men and women', not immaterial parts of men and women. Nevertheless, these animal bodies do have an immaterial part, which is the subject/agent of experience. The immaterial part is, as Descartes himself said, so interfused and compounded with the body that soul and body form one thing: 'I am not just lodged in my body like a pilot in his ship, but ... I am intimately united with it, and so confused and intermingled with it that I and my body compose, as it were, a single whole' (*Meditations*, 6). Thomas Aquinas allowed that human souls ('intellectual souls') might exist without bodies, but if they did so, they would exist 'in an unnatural and imperfect way'

(*Summa Theologiae*).[7] For humans are meant to be soul-body compound beings.

This insistence on the importance of a material body to the human soul does not involve a renunciation of idealism. It is true to say that human souls are produced by bodies, in that they are emergent complexes of phenomenal data and intellectual capacities, together with the continuing subjects of such data and of such capacities. However, it does seem inconceivable that material bodies, with only properties such as mass, spin, charge, position, and momentum, could actually by their own powers bring mental properties into existence. But it is conceivable that the basic physical laws and constants of the cosmos could be so set up that when physical structures become sufficiently integrated and complex, a potential for conscious intelligence which has always been present in some sense will be realised. This does seem to suppose a teleological structure to the physical universe, and a cosmic mind which could envisage and realise such a complex interplay of potentialities and natural powers. This is just what believers in God think, accepting that bodies and souls are both produced and sustained in being by God, so that they could not exist without the one ultimate Mind of all things. Obviously this form of idealism does not deny the existence of matter; it is not 'immaterialism'. But it affirms that matter as it is known to us is shaped by our minds, and that matter in itself only exists as an expression of the mind of God. We might say that God, matter, and souls all exist. But finite minds and bodies are essentially expressions of God, from whom they arise and to whom they are destined to return.

Christians sometimes point out that the New Testament does not just speak of bodies and souls, for St. Paul seemed to speak of a

----

[7] Thomas Aquinas, *Summa Theologiae* 1a, question 76, article 1.

threefold complexity in humans: body (*soma*), soul (*psyche*), and spirit (*pneuma*).[8] This is true, and Paul was perhaps thinking of the Greek threefold division of body, soul, and reason (*nous*). On this account, the soul or mind is regarded as the part of the mind that engages with perception and is concerned with the sensory world. It is rather like what German philosophers, especially Kant, called 'Understanding' (*Verstehen*), which for Kant imposes its categories of thought on the data of the senses and sees those data as appearances of enduring objects in causal relation to one another. *Nous* is intellect or reason, the mind insofar as it is concerned with non-sensory realities, usually of a more intellectual nature. It is what may contemplate Platonic forms. Though Kant gave up the idea that the mind can actually contemplate existing intelligible realities, he regarded 'Reason' (*Vernunft*) as an essential and important human capacity that constrains how humans must think of the intelligible world, the world beyond phenomenal appearances. For Kant, who disliked any idea of actual experience of God – and even more so for Hegel, who thought that religion was only a picturesque way of talking about a purely rational reality – Reason was concerned with the intelligible realm of pure ideas, ideas which could not find a specific instantiation in the sensory world.

I think that Christians, who generally have a more devotional relation to a more personal God, might rather think of 'Spirit' as mind in loving relation to God. Thus soul and spirit are not different sorts of things. They are more like differing functions of the mind – one in relation to the sensory world and its structures, and the other in relation to objective values and to the personal reality of God. We can see that the human spirit and the divine Spirit, meeting in loving embrace, may be hard to distinguish, and

---

[8] For instance, 1 Thessalonians 5, 23.

so Christians sometimes speak of a union between them, where one might say, with Paul, 'It is no longer I who live, but it is Christ who lives in me' (Galatians 2, 20). My spirit is enfolded and enlightened by the Spirit of Christ. Or we might say that the human mind and the divine mind are naturally shaped to complement each other. This may seem a long way beyond empiricism, but actually it is for Christians a natural and fitting interpretation of the human situation. Human knowledge begins with experience, and that experience includes the felt agency of a continuing self, the subject of experiences and the agent of intentional actions. This is what Christian theologians have traditionally called the soul, which is related both to the physical world in which it is embodied and to the non-physical reality of God which is its creator and sustainer.

CHAPTER 5

Inferential and Interpretative Hypotheses

Idealists have the same starting point as empiricists. But idealists differ among themselves about the exact relation of mental contents to an objective physical reality. Berkeley notoriously denied that there was any physical reality (though his view is rather more sophisticated than he is often given credit for). Kant held that we must posit such a reality but that we cannot know its true nature. Hegel held that Reason can know the nature of reality and that it is basically *Geist*, or Absolute Spirit – certainly not material. And there are other possibilities. What is agreed among idealists is that experience is real and is not reducible to matter. Experience must form the starting point of enquiry into the nature of reality. Experiences need to be attended to, linked in a series of uniquely unified elements, and interpreted as appearances of an objective reality, and so they presuppose the existence of thinking minds. Without mind, there will be no value or purpose in the universe. If we believe that there is value and purpose in the universe, something mind-like may well be the basis of physical reality, and without that mind-like reality, there would exist nothing at all.

Almost all believers in God are idealists in some sense. Christian theists believe that God created the universe through Wisdom (the *Logos* of John chapter 1), that the universe is good (of value), that there is a purpose in creation (that intelligent beings should know God and enjoy God forever), and that human minds are made 'in the image' of the Creator (so God is not totally unlike human minds). Thus they certainly wish to say that value and purpose exist in the universe and are fundamental to its existence. They are committed to believing in a supreme consciousness which lays down the basic laws of nature so that nature is intelligible and reliable in its operations. Consciousness, value, and purpose do not just arise, Christians will say, as if by accident, when humans come into existence, millions of years after the beginning of the universe. They have always been implicit in the constitution of the physical universe, and the incredible development of physical integrated complexity which brings central nervous systems and brains into existence is purposefully aimed at the generation of finite minds.

If we accept that consciousness – the existence of perceptions, thoughts, feelings, memories, and intentions – is a basic feature of reality and that our belief in an objective reality is an inference or postulate (a well-confirmed one) from conscious experiences, then we can overcome the modern prejudice that the existence of matter is more obvious than the existence of spiritual (or mind-like) things. And we might see that the postulate of one supreme consciousness (God) is not so very different in its logical character from the postulate of an objective physical world.

In this way empiricism very naturally leads to belief in the priority of consciousness, which naturally leads to belief in God. Yet well-known empiricists like David Hume and A. J. (Freddie) Ayer were certainly not believers in God. Of course empiricists do not have to believe in God. It is possible to say that conscious experiences are real, and involve value and purpose, but it does not follow that there is one supreme conscious experience which gives value and purpose to the whole universe. It does not follow, even, that there is an objective physical world which exists apart from our experiences. Hume appeared to think that reason could not establish such a thing, and we just have to rely on common sense (i.e. basic belief) to support the view that there is. He thought that common sense assumed the existence of a physical world but not the existence of God. As his Scottish contemporary Thomas Reid pointed out, common sense could equally well support the view that there is a God. It all depends on whose common sense you are consulting.

Freddie Ayer argued that belief in an external physical world is indeed a hypothesis which cannot be directly confirmed by any experience. In later life he came to agree that God too is such a hypothesis.[1] But he thought that the hypothesis of a physical world is necessary for us to make sense of what would otherwise just be a confusing jumble of experiences. The hypothesis of God, he thought, is not needed to make sense of experience, and it is indeed vacuous, adding nothing of substance or practical usefulness to the sum of human knowledge. In fact, he thought the idea of God was actually misleading and harmful, leading people to unrealistic expectations about prayers beings answered or miracles occurring, for example, and sometimes leading them to kill those who disagreed with them.

In considering this claim, it might be useful to distinguish between an inferential hypothesis and what might be called an interpretative hypothesis. An inferential hypothesis is one that explains some observed phenomenon by postulating an unperceived, or even unperceivable, entity or state. A good example is the hypothesis that this universe began with a 'Big Bang', a sudden

---

[1] Ayer conceded, in *The Central Questions of Philosophy* (Weidenfeld and Nicolson, 1973), that the verification principle ran into pretty insuperable difficulties (p. 27), so for the word 'God' to be meaningful, God did not have to be an object of sense experience. But he thought that there were great difficulties in making the concept of God internally coherent, and that in any case it had no explanatory force. I am, of course, seeking to provide a coherent concept and to show what sort of explanatory force it has.

inflation or expansion from a primal point of virtually infinite energy. This is a very well-established hypothesis, accepted by almost all physicists. But the Big Bang is not perceivable even in principle. It has to be inferred from observations like the cosmic microwave background and the red shift of expanding star systems.

An interpretative hypothesis, on the other hand, is one that interprets some experienced reality in terms of concepts that do not derive simply from the observations in themselves. The hypothesis introduces concepts that enable perceived data to be interpreted in a particular way. The best example is the hypothesis that there is a world of continuing and causally related physical objects. The objects are perceived and are not just hidden entities. Yet there is something hidden about them, and they are the results of thought, not of simple perception.

Immanuel Kant is the philosopher who tried to work out this conception in the most detail. Even though his analysis, in the *Critique of Pure Reason*, is almost certainly too artificially systematic, I believe that he is successful in showing that there are certain concepts (like the concepts of causality and substance) that are necessary conditions of the possibility of knowledge of objects. We interpret our sense perceptions by using the concept of a world of physical objects in causal interaction. We do not say that we first perceive sense-data and then use concepts to interpret them as appearances of independently existing objects. Rather, we use the concepts (what he calls the 'categories') in such a way that from the first it seems to us that what we perceive are the appearances of physical objects.[2]

Thus we can say that we perceive physical objects as they appear to us. We really see the objects, and not something else.

---

[2] Kant, *Critique of Pure Reason* (1781), 'Transcendental Analytic'.

Nevertheless, what we see are the appearances of objects, and the objects in themselves, as they are when not being perceived by us, remain unperceivable. This is more than a mere tautology, for we have very good reasons – mostly derived from scientific study – for saying that unperceived physical objects are very different from their appearances to us (on one scientific account, they may be probability waves in eleven dimensions, for example).

The postulate of an external physical world is an interpretative hypothesis. It posits that there is an unperceivable world of physical objects, but this is not just an inference concerning totally unperceived entities. For we do perceive those entities, though only inasmuch as they appear to us. To other possible observers, they may appear differently. Nevertheless, for us they are genuine appearances of real physical objects, not just illusions.

The distinction between appearance and reality is crucial. For philosophers like Kant (who called himself a 'transcendental' or 'critical' idealist[3]), the perceived world is not an illusion. But the world as appearance is the world as it is expressed in a certain way to a specific set of observing beings. Conscious experiences are real (not just half-real, as Plato sometimes said). They give genuine knowledge of an objective reality. But reality as it is in itself is not identical with reality as we perceive it. There is an objective reality, but its inner nature is not perceivable by us.

Largely because of the impressive success of modern science, there is a tendency to think that reality-in-itself is the world

---

[3] Immanuel Kant, *Prolegomena* (1783), 'First Part of the General Transcendental Problem – How Is Pure Mathematic Possible?' In Remark I Kant says that his view is 'the very opposite of idealism'. But by idealism here he means that nothing exists but thinking beings, a view he takes to be that of Berkeley and to be absurd, 'mystical and visionary'. In remark III he makes it clear that he is an idealist, though of a different sort – what in the First Critique he called 'transcendental idealism' but of which term he now says, 'I now retract it, and desire this idealism of mine to be called critical'. In other words, he believes that appearances are not objective things, though he does think objective things exist. Whether this is as different from Berkeley as he supposes is not as clear as he thinks.

described by science. But Kant's question, from which the whole complex argument of his *Critique of Pure Reason* began, remains: how do we know that our knowledge corresponds with external reality? His answer was that we can never know that. The best we can do is to say that what we call reality is based on concepts that we ourselves generate and that are justified by the fact that they are necessary conditions of the possibility of the sort of interpretations of experiences that we find it necessary to use in practice. This Kant called, in the first Critique, 'transcendental idealism'. It is necessary for the sort of relation to external reality that we have. But it does not reveal the inner nature of things-in-themselves.

On this account, the world view of science is an abstraction from the world view of common sense.[4] It virtually eliminates all traces of consciousness, value, and purpose from its picture of reality. It constructs a mathematical schema that is useful for understanding why things happen as they do in our experienced world. It reveals what we might call the mathematical skeleton of the world as appearance, and as such it has proved to be of immense practical utility. But it does not reveal the structure of reality-in-itself. That structure must, if it is to be adequate and comprehensive, somehow include all the manifold data of conscious perception and experience as well as the data of experimentally controlled observation, devoid of passion and sentiment, which it is the goal of physics to provide.

Human relations to reality are not confined to experimentally controlled and publicly repeatable observations. In fact, such observations are very rare and require sophisticated mathematical and technological advances before they become possible for humans. If

---

[4] Niels Bohr, one of the originators of quantum theory, wrote to a friend, 'There is no quantum world. There is only abstract quantum physical description' (quoted in M. Jammer, *The Philosophy of Quantum Theory*, Wiley, 1974, p. 204).

we examine the nature of human conscious experience, and see it as an interaction with a reality that appears to us in various ways, we find many other aspects of such human interaction than the scientific. These aspects must all be taken into account if we are to provide a truly comprehensive account of human knowledge and belief. In Chapter 6, I will outline four key areas of human experience that will have their place in any such account, and I will try to show that the idea of God is a reasonable and natural interpretative hypothesis that helps us integrate these into a coherent whole. Just as the postulate of an objective physical world helps make sense of sense perceptions, so the postulate of something like God helps make sense of the wider range of human experience, which is constituted of personal feelings, values, and purposes, as well as of publicly testable intelligible laws of nature.

CHAPTER 6

The Objectivity of Value

I have argued that minds have a place in experienced reality that cannot be reduced to non-mental, or purely physical, realities. I now wish to point to four important areas of experience – without holding that these are the only important areas there are – which suggest that values are objective constituents of reality as it is experienced. The idea of God, as a supreme mind, can be seen as a fruitful interpretative hypothesis for seeing and responding to such values as we experience them in these different ways.

First is our understanding of the physical world. Scientific investigation has shown that the basic structure of that world is mathematically elegant and beautiful, that the world is ordered in accordance with a few simple principles (the laws and constants of nature), and that entities develop amazingly complex and integrated forms as they evolve over billions of years from an initial undifferentiated primordial state. Seen in this way, the natural world is an object of awe, as it produces manifold beautiful forms in accordance with stable and intelligible principles.

It is possible to just stop there, with a recognition of the amazing structure of the cosmos. It is even possible, as we have seen, to hold that the mathematical, impersonal, and unconscious principles of the natural order are the ultimate reality which accounts for the existence of everything else. But a natural response to our recognition of the intelligibility of nature is to see it as an appearance or

expression of some underlying wisdom or intelligence: 'The heavens are telling the glory of God; and the firmament proclaims his
handiwork' (Psalm 19, 1). This is not a naive idea that there is some
invisible person, whose existence would stand in need of further
explanation, making things happen in the cosmos. Nor is it some
sort of demonstrative proof of God which no intelligent person
could deny. Rather, it is seeing the cosmos as an expression of
immense power and wisdom – in the way that we might see the
bodily actions of others as an expression of their fully embodied
personalities. We are not inferring to an unknown but separate and
invisible person. We are interpreting what we see and understand
as a reality of almost incredible elegance and integrated complexity.
Seen thus, the universe speaks of intelligence and mind, but it is a
mind expressed in the physical structure, not some separate quite
well understood person working behind the scenes. At the same
time, we are aware that this expressed intelligence is an appearance
of an unknown reality. We know it as expression; there is a
transcendent depth to our understanding of it. For theists, the
word 'God' denotes (in part) this transcendent depth. But whether
or not we use the word 'God', our form of apprehension inherently
points beyond itself to the veiled reality which it partially reveals.
It is an interpretative hypothesis for marking the way we see and
understand this aspect of reality.

There are other aspects of our apprehension of reality that are
important. The second one I shall mention is the sense of the
beautiful in the arts and in the natural world. It is possible to hear
a great piece of music or to see a beautiful painting and remain quite
unmoved. If so, we fail to see the most important thing about it. We
fail to see what the sounds or coloured shapes convey to those who
are sensitive to them. It is virtually impossible to describe in words
what is conveyed. Even though music and art criticism can be

helpful in teaching us what to look for and appreciate, such criticism can also sometimes descend into verbose nonsense as it tries to express in words what only truly lives in pure sounds and pigments.

In music, all there is, physically, is electromagnetic wavelengths causing the firing of neurons in the brain. Even phenomenally, in sounds heard, there are only sounds of a specific timbre, force, and pitch. But music carries so much more, and that more is what is supremely important. It is what is conveyed by the sounds — something that can stir deep emotions, something that expresses the peculiar creativity of the composer and that is meant to give pleasure of a particular aesthetic, non-sensory sort.

Art expresses creative insight, an individual perspective on the world which the sounds or shapes convey and that can, and is meant to, move the hearer to 'feel' the world in a certain way. Those feelings are not meant to be purely subjective tingles or sensations that carry no informative content. They are feelings with content, feelings that open up aspects of the world and of human existence that we may not otherwise have perceived. Those aspects are unspoken. They are played, drawn, or danced — activities that communicate information non-verbally. They become evocative symbols of a veiled reality that is shaped by creative endeavour and that is perceived by sensitive response.

Art opens up aspects of reality that can be apprehended by feeling. But, as in perception, what is perceived remains appearance, an expression of a reality always beyond and ungraspable by thought. In creativity we feel that reality shaping our construction of sensory symbols. In artistic appreciation we receive those symbols into ourselves, and with their aid we construct our own response to the veiled reality of which we are part.

It is not surprising that a natural reaction to many aspects of nature is similarly one of encountering sensory data that point beyond themselves and become symbols of transcendent beauty. Different people feel these things to different degrees – some overwhelmingly and some not at all. We see in nature sublime beauty, but we also see terror and power that dwarfs us into insignificance.

Not all observers would use the concept of 'God' in this context – largely because of other connotations of that word which they may not attune with.[1] Yet such apprehensions of transcendent beauty and terrifying power are a major root of the idea of 'God'. Rudolf Otto, in *Das Heilige*,[2] even defined God largely in terms of experiences of, on the one hand, admiration and desire and, on the other, terror and dread. The *'tremendum et fascinans'* of which he spoke was an interpretation of the natural word as expressive and symbolic of what lies beyond. This 'beyond' was not an anthropomorphic person, but rather the nature of the Real as expressed in the creative and destructive powers of nature, powers which are inextricably bound together in the deep structure of the cosmos.

On this understanding, God is irresistible Beauty and terrifying Power, a transcendent reality expressed in aspects of the natural world and also in the creative and appreciative activity of human minds. The affective responses which such aspects evoke tell us something about the reality of which we are parts, and they can be more or less deep and illuminating. Christians do not have to look far to find such responses present throughout the Biblical record. The God of Mount Sinai, hidden in a cloud of darkness yet expressed in a still small voice, and the God whose beauty is seen in the person of Jesus and whose power is seen in Jesus' resurrection from the dead is a God whose nature is shown throughout

---

[1] A good example of this is Iris Murdoch, who, in *The Sovereignty of Good* (Routledge, 1970), writes beautifully of how art communicates what she calls 'the Good' but insists that this is not to be identified with God, whom, she thinks, is an interfering busybody with specific causal powers in the physical world.

[2] Rudolf Otto (1917, trans. as *The Idea of the Holy*, Oxford University Press, 1923).

creation. That nature can be dangerous and terrible, and it can be supremely beautiful ('glorious'). To delight in the beauty of the world and to stand in awe before the sheer power of nature – both are parts of that 'fear of the Lord' which is the beginning of wisdom.

In the beauty and the awesome power of nature and in human creativity we can sense the presence of objective values where the purely physical seems to point beyond itself to a transcendent depth.[3] But an even more important aspect of reality is the existence of moral values. The sense that there are moral values or ideals that exist and that exert a psychological pressure on us to try to realise them in our lives is a third important aspect of human experience. For some people morality is little more than a set of social conventions or rules for obtaining some degree of security in society. But, as Immanuel Kant emphasised, there is a sense of duty as something which is absolutely binding on us, whatever our desires happen to be. The basic rules of the Ten Commandments – do not kill, do not steal, do not lie, and do not commit adultery – are not just conventions. They are principles which bind us to obedience, even when we are tempted to kill or lie for what we might think are good reasons. Why should we live by such principles? The truly moral answer, many people would say, is that those principles are objectively binding. We do not just make them up; we apprehend their force. They are principles which define our humanity as beings under obligation to support life, liberty, truth, and loyalty. Whereas we often are tempted to seek our own pleasure and position above those of others, morality counsels us to set aside selfishness and pursue what is good for its own sake.

---

[3] Fiona Ellis, in *God, Values, and Nature* (Oxford University Press, 2014), argues for what she calls an 'expansive naturalism' – the view that values exist objectively in the natural world. This requires that 'natural' not be interpreted narrowly, as 'that which is measurable by the natural sciences'. She explicitly suggests, too, that this form of naturalism can be so expanded as to include God – a move to which the present chapter is very sympathetic.

How can something as abstract as 'morality' do that? Where is morality anyway, and how can it exist? Even those who do not believe in God can know and feel that they ought to seek truth and the well-being of others, and that being truly human is being committed to the pursuit of such ideals. But it is hard to say why that should be so if humans are mere accidental by-products of a meaningless universe whose best efforts will probably fail in the long run anyway.

Belief in God enables us to say that there is a Being who has created us precisely in order that we should be loving and truthful, even in a world where hatred and lies have become, through the free choices of intelligent beings, commonplace. In the sense of moral obligation – the sense that some acts are right for their own sake and some states are worth aiming at for their own sake – we are able to perceive the purpose of our lives.[4] If there is such a purpose, then we may hope that despite all our seeming failures that purpose will finally be realised, not through our own power but through a power greater than our own. So God can give to morality an objective reality and depth which strengthens and motivates us. Morality will not be seen as just a set of man-made conventions. It will be part of the deepest fabric of reality, and in pursuing the good we will be fulfilling the purpose of our lives.

It would be a caricature to say that God is brought in as some sort of external sovereign who just issues commands and forces us to obey them. That is the wrong place to start. What we must do is sense the force and power of moral ideals and principles – the states that are worthwhile for their own sakes and the principles that we cannot disobey without losing our true humanity. We may then come to feel that these are not fictions. They are parts of objective

---

[4] I argue for this position more fully in *Morality, Autonomy, and God* (Oneworld Press, 2013).

reality; they are built into the way things are. That means that the reality we apprehend is more than the unconscious machinations of subatomic particles. Reality contains objective values, which attract and constrain us and define our very nature as free moral agents.

These apprehensions of moral value are appearances in our consciousness of features that objectively exist in reality. They point beyond themselves to values as parts of the nature of the objectively real. It is a plausible suggestion, and it seems to me to be true, that values only really exist when they are consciously known and valued, when they are the contents of some consciousness that can appreciate them and wish them to be values for other conscious beings also. Values which are not recognised as such can be seen as features of reality that ought to be valued, but as such they remain potential rather than actual. Their potentiality is only realised when they are consciously recognised, and the way in which they are recognised, interpreted, and appreciated gives a distinctive form to their actuality. In this sense it is possible to say that objective values are actual in their fullest form only when rooted in a supreme consciousness, the consciousness of God. For finite minds they remain ideals to be realised by disciplined attention. Potential for us, they are actual in God, and in loving those values we in fact love the God whose nature defines what they are and makes them normative for our own, dependent lives. In this way moral experience is a distinctive aspect of human consciousness which opens up to us access to another greater mind of infinitely greater value. Seen in this way, moral value opens up to us the mind of God.

CHAPTER 7

Personal Knowledge

Our ordinary experience of the world does not disclose a purely physical reality. It discloses values of intelligibility, creativity, beauty, and goodness. These aspects of reality are known in experience, as we see and interpret that experience and respond to it as to a veiled yet possibly mind-like reality that is expressed in many diverse human experiences. All these features are included, integrated within, and completed by a fourth element of human experience: the sense of personal presence which enables us to see other people as not just bundles of atoms, but as thinking and feeling, intelligent, and responsible agents. This sense, or something closely analogous to it, is characteristic of what is often called religious experience, though I have tried to stress that experience of God ranges much more widely than over these often rather rare and distinctive experiences.

The sense of personal presence is well known to all of us. We have such a sense when we are in the presence of another human person. Even when they do not speak or move, we may have a strong sense of their presence with us, and that sense may irradiate and transform all our consciousness. I think it would be totally inadequate to say that the sense of the personal is just an inference from observed behaviour, as though minds were hidden entities known only in their effects. As the Oxford philosopher Cook Wilson said, 'We don't want merely inferred friends.' When we meet other persons physically, we have a direct apprehension of their personal nature. Their bodies are not just the basis for inferences – we could never establish that such an inference was correct, as its 'hidden term' could never be observed. Their bodies mediate their personhood; they are appearances that point beyond themselves, but they are interpreted by us from the first as the expressions of a distinctively personal reality. Such a reality has an inner life and agency, and a reality which is conveyed to others precisely in and through its physical appearances.

For vast numbers of humans, that sense of the personal is not confined to human bodies. The Jewish thinker Martin Buber has called it the 'I-Thou' relationship and finds it in a wide range of human experiences.[1]

Some of those engaged in the cognitive sciences have posited what Justin Barrett has called a 'Hyperactive agent detection device – HADD'. They argue that early humans developed a natural tendency to regard almost all objects as personal, as animated by desires and purposes. This, he argued, helped them avoid danger, as it was better to think something was attacking you and that you were about to be eaten rather than to get eaten before you had decided whether or not there really was an agent there.[2]

Most Christians (and Justin Barrett is a Christian, as it happens) might agree that there is such a natural tendency to see the personal in many parts of the natural world. But they might not see that tendency as primarily a product of the fear of predators. It may be a feeling of affinity with the natural world and a recognition of dependence upon a nature which has produced humans and

[1] Martin Buber, *I and Thou* (trans. Ronald Gregor Smith, T and T Clark, 1958 – first published 1923).
[2] Justin L. Barrett, *Cognitive Science, Religion, and Theology* (Templeton Press, 2011), gives a brief and helpful account of how the cognitive science of religion impacts on belief in God, and he suggests that the sense of personal presence that is so marked in many humans can reasonably be seen as implanted by a God who desires that people should naturally be able to relate to God in love and devotion.

supports their existence. And why should that feeling be 'hyper-active'? If the cosmos is an appearance of a mind-like reality, it is not strange that a sense of that mind should be evoked by parts of the natural world.

Humans have often regarded mountains, streams, and woods as sacred places, with their own unique character that can be felt by those who are sensitive to it. Joseph Conrad's novels speak of ships that carry a distinctive atmosphere and feeling, and many of us are familiar with places that seem 'creepy' or capable of evoking feelings of unity with all things, or of dependence upon a more sublime reality – what Schleiermacher called a 'sense of the infinite', conveyed through finite elements of experience.[3]

Some of the most intelligent and morally sensitive people in history have experienced such a sense. Christians, among them Brother Lawrence, call it the sense of the presence of God. Christians have felt it especially evoked by the person of Christ, but it can also be experienced in many parts of life, when the world suddenly appears as a veil drawn aside for a moment to reveal its inner nature as always transcendent and yet as apprehensible by us as we learn to be attentive to it.

This sense of the personal can be found at the heart of many religious traditions. In Buddhism it can appear as the presence of a Bodhisattva, a compassionate being who saves devotees from the three fires of hatred, greed, and ignorance. Sometimes, as in some Chinese traditions, it appears as the Tao – the 'Way' of harmony and balance that rules in the heavens and that should rule in

---

[3] Friedrich Schleiermacher, in *On Religion: Speeches to Its Cultured Despisers* (trans. Richard Crouter, Cambridge University Press, 1988 – first published 1799), second speech. Schleiermacher rooted 'religious piety' in what he later called the 'sense of absolute dependence', not in doctrine or ethics. It needs stressing, however, that this was no subjective inner sensation; it was an acquaintance with an objective reality – which he variously called 'the infinite', 'the one', or 'the absolutely independent'. It is, of course, God.

society – apprehension of which can deliver humans from the wheel of suffering. In some forms of Hinduism, Krishna or Shiva are images which symbolise and embody in finite forms the infinite being of the consciousness, intelligence, and bliss (*sat-Cit-Ananda*) which is the true nature of all things in their ultimate unity.

In these ways, idealists see the mind of the cosmos appearing to humans in ways that are culture-dependent and subject to historical development. It looks as if 'revelations' or disclosures of the cosmic do not generally take the form of infallible and unchangeable propositional utterances. Apprehensions of the personal are interpreted in forms which have developed in particular histories and cultures. For instance, the idea of a 'Way of Heaven' (*Tian*) is very different from the idea of a liberated state beyond human individuality (*Nirvana*). But both traditions share the idea of something objective, beyond humanity, and of great value, apprehension of which by enlightened minds suggests a true way of living as persons in this cosmos. Whether it is called personal or not depends partly on whether individual personhood is valued in the culture in question, but basic reality is endowed with moral properties which are certainly not purely physical in nature. These realities are non-material, though they may be closely associated or intertwined with the material realm (the idea of a harmony of nature can hardly exist where there is no nature). In this sense we might speak of a sense of the spiritual aspects of the world of human experience – aspects connected with ideas of value and purpose, of states worth aiming at, and objective ideals for living a good human life.

It is in the Abrahamic religious traditions, beginning with early Hebrew faith, that the idea of a personal will who is an intentional creator of the cosmos develops in its clearest form. The personal presence underlying all experience is seen as having knowledge and intentions, and as having a good purpose for the physical world.

Christians belong to this set of traditions, and what chiefly distinguishes Christian faith is its claim that the creator God has revealed the divine nature and purpose, not solely but most fully, and indeed decisively, in Jesus of Nazareth. In Jesus, God is disclosed as self-giving (*agapistic*) love, and that love has the purpose of liberating humans from evil and uniting them to the divine, in which condition their human lives can be fulfilled.

The faith that human nature can be transfigured so that it becomes one with the divine nature, and that the divine nature is compassionate love, is the Gospel of Jesus. His message, as I understand it, was that the kingdom of God (the rule of God) has come close to humans and that God's purpose is to bring all human lives which respond positively into an unbreakable friendship with God. The sense of God which Christians experience is the apprehension of a life-transforming and life-fulfilling wisdom, beauty, and goodness which gradually forms from the rather unpromising material of ambiguous humanity a communion of perfected love.[4]

If, in philosophy, we start from perceptions which are from the first interpreted by thought and apprehended through feeling, then we will not be tempted to reduce reality to just a set of dispassionately observed sensory data. For some extreme empiricists, sensory data is all there is ('the world is the totality of facts' said Wittgenstein in the *Tractatus Logico-Philosophicus*, which he spent the rest of his philosophical life amending) – just streams of perceptions strung together without rhyme or reason, with no connections of necessity or coherence between them. But the fact is that perceptions do form a coherent and intelligible whole. It is thought which discerns that intelligible reality and feeling that

---

[4] I explore this theological theme in what is a companion volume to this one, *Christ and the Cosmos* (Cambridge University Press, 2016).

apprehends its inner nature in and through the sensory appearances in which it is expressed.

There is thus much more to reality than that with which the natural sciences deal. Yet the natural sciences too, when they are fully appreciated, disclose transcendent depths to the reality that they investigate. The sciences uncover the deep intelligibility of the world, and a feeling for science is a feeling for the complex elegance and rich variety of the reality it unveils. It is, in my view, a pathology of scientific understanding to think that its invaluable techniques of mathematical abstraction and of the reductive analysis of complex entities into their elementary components uncover the whole of what reality is. Such reduction leaves reality without sentience, value, or purpose and pictures the elegant intricacy of the laws of nature as just accidental facts that have come together by chance. Those who truly love science because they love the beauty and structure of the natural world know better. They know that science is the poetry of nature. They know that the whole of nature does not exist just to produce a few human beings or beetles. It exists for its own sake – or, better, for the sake of the understanding and appreciation of its manifold forms which the cosmos makes possible for the mind that underlies and is expressed in it. As Charles Darwin put it, in the final sentence of *The Origin of Species*, 'There is grandeur in this view of life ... from so simple a beginning endless forms most beautiful and most wonderful have been, and are being, evolved.'[5] There is a place for feeling and value in science, and those who would be scientists will be most attracted to it by that sense of beauty and wonder which our understanding of the cosmos inspires.

Steven Weinberg was thus misleadingly pessimistic when he said, 'The more the universe seems comprehensible, the more it

---

[5] Charles Darwin, *The Origin of Species*, 1859.

also seems pointless' (*The First Three Minutes*).[6] For the understanding of the universe, and the feeling for its beauty and wonder, is precisely the point of it. That understanding is perhaps only fully found in the mind of its Creator. But, by thought and feeling, by effort and application, it can be developed also in human minds.

We apprehend beauty and wonder in the world through the study of the sciences and the arts. We also apprehend, in morality, values and ideals which inspire our actions. And we can apprehend the presence of the personal, both in other humans and in the natural order, which can be signs of a universal mind that contains and generates intelligibility, beauty, and goodness, and is the reality both veiled and revealed in human perceptions and experiences.

Ayer found the idea of God a vacuous explanation for why things are as they are. But that was because he did not discern intelligibility, beauty, and value as objective features of the world. Such things were, he thought, purely subjective ideas in human minds. The reason why the idea of God is not a vacuous explanation is because positing an underlying mind-like reality that is expressed in the cosmos explains how intelligibility, beauty, and value can be found in objective reality. For these are not material properties; they are properties which properly exist in relation to minds which can apprehend and appreciate them. The mind that fully apprehends the intelligibility, beauty, and value of the cosmos is no limited human mind. Humans do not project or impose such properties upon a neutral backdrop of sense-data. They apprehend them as elements of reality which claim attention and response, and which can change and refashion human subjective judgments as humans learn to attend to what is real in more appropriate ways.

---

[6] Steven Weinberg, *The First Three Minutes* (Andre Deutsch, 1977), p. 149.

It is true that religious sensibility can lead to superstition and fanaticism, when it is not subject to a rigorous use of rational and morally sensitive reflection. But Christians have usually supposed, and are logically obliged to suppose, that the God who created the cosmos through the *Logos* is supremely rational and that the God who suffered in human form for the sake of human salvation is supremely good. God is an explanatory hypothesis, but an interpretative one, not an inferential one. The interpretation of the cosmos as the expression of a supreme mind replaces the sense that we are lonely specks of awareness in an alien and uncaring cosmos with a realisation that we are minds always in communion with a supreme mind that meets and enfolds us in all the unique experiences of our lives. That is no vacuous speculation. It makes possible a total transformation of every human experience.

PART II

Eternal Mind

CHAPTER 8

The Idea of an Ultimate Mind

In the first part of this book, having begun by outlining the philosophy of personal idealism, I argued that the obvious starting place for human knowledge is conscious experience. Sense perceptions, thoughts, and feelings, are different in kind from spatially located, publicly observable objects, and they have a distinctive and irreducible reality. I went on to claim that human experience includes as an essential component the idea of a unitary subject-self, the owner of experiences. This subject-self is known as a continuing agent both in thought and in bodily actions, and it is what makes humans free and responsible agents. It is what Christians, and most believers in God, speak of as 'the soul' – the continuing owner and agent of human life experiences.

Looking more fully at the nature of thought, I introduced the idea of interpretative hypotheses, which provide interpretative categories enabling subjects to see their experiences as giving knowledge of an objectively existing world. I proposed that the scientific world view as it is found in modern physics is an abstract mathematical schema and that the common-sense world view is in fact a complex intellectual construction which is, in Kantian terms, a condition of the possibility of objective knowledge of the world as appearance, the inner nature of which remains a largely 'veiled reality'. However, in experience there are many signs of transcendence where the veil is at least partly drawn aside. I mentioned specifically science, the arts,

73

morality, and encounter with persons as areas of human experience and activity in which intimations of objective purpose and value can be found. Thus the experienced world gives rise to the idea of objective values which encounter and challenge human agents. That notion of objective value and purpose can evoke a sense of one supreme Mind in which objective values and purposes can be rooted.

In this second part I will explore further the idea of a supreme mind-like foundation for reality (what idealists often call 'Spirit' and what theists call God) and argue that the idea has real explanatory power, that it is wholly consistent with and supportive of modern science, and that it is a strong philosophical foundation for Christian belief.

Minds are real. They are, as I have described them, partly self-directing streams of experience. If so, the hard materialist theory that we are nothing more than bits of matter arranged in complicated ways is false. We are something more than that, and the 'more' is the most important thing about us. But of course human minds are embodied in matter. They are not in some quite different hidden world, only connected to matter by strange invisible wires. Minds are not 'ghosts in a machine', as the philosopher Gilbert Ryle described them (in *The Concept of Mind*, 1949).[1] They are generated from brains and might be regarded as the 'inner side' of matter, when matter is arranged in very complex, organised ways. In human beings, minds seem to emerge from matter, even though their properties are not the properties of ordinary matter.

Consciousness, value, and purpose do, in human beings, somehow emerge from matter, and I do not think anyone has quite worked out how this happens or what the relationship between mind and matter is.

---

[1] Once long ago, Gilbert Ryle was my philosophy tutor, and I have had the temerity to criticise his view of mind in my *More Than Matter?* (Lion Hudson, 2010).

Many modern philosophers have a particular animus against Rene Descartes, and 'Cartesian dualism' is often used as a term of abuse. This view is usually described as one which makes an absolute distinction of kind between mind and matter. Matter is a mechanical, deterministic, valueless, purposeless set of substances extended in space with only such properties as mass, position, and velocity. Mind, on the other hand, consists of private extensionless substances which think, feel, and act purposively. Mind and matter are connected contingently and in a mysterious way, and it is very hard to see how purpose and awareness can interact with the deterministic and law-governed world of material substances.

I doubt whether this is a fair or full account of Descartes' thought, but he certainly said things which gave rise to this 'Cartesian' account of the relation of mind and matter.[2] It may seem that my own account of minds or souls as continuing and partly self-directing streams of experience verges on this sort of Cartesian dualism. I do indeed think that there can be mental content (thoughts and images) which could exist without being embodied in a physical brain and environment. But I do not think that human persons are or should be disembodied. Human sentience and intelligence emerge from complex integrated physical structures. They are not optional extras added to a physical reality which is completely explicable in purely physical terms.

Human minds, as continuing centres of action and experience, are aspects of complex structures, and minds have causal powers which are not just the sum of the physical structures from which they arise and in which they are embodied. Thus the idea of a purely material world is an abstraction and selection from a much richer reality which contains values and purposes as well as

[2] A very good account of Descartes' thought is given by John Cottingham in *Cartesian Reflections* (Oxford University Press, 2008). He shows that Descartes was not a 'dualist' in a crude 'two distinct worlds' sense and that the popular animus against 'Cartesian dualism' does not give a fair account of Descartes' wholly theistic thought.

positions and velocities. Minds are aspects of a unitary reality which realises possibilities that have always been inherent in it, as it progressively realises its potencies through generating a relational web of finite centres of consciousness and action.

This is a central thesis of idealism, and I want to affirm that the material world itself is essentially a product of mind, which is the opposite of what seems to be the case with human minds. One may ask, 'How could mind produce matter?' But in reality that question, and the possible responses to it, is no more peculiar or puzzling than the question 'How could matter produce minds?' One process seems no harder to explain than the other. Both are pretty mysterious to us, but to me at least it is easier to think of a supreme mind conceiving of possible universes from which finite minds could emerge, and then bringing one or more such universes into being, than to think of blind, unconscious, and apparently rule-bound matter suddenly, unforeseeably, and unexpectedly producing conscious and intelligent beings.

It is nevertheless obvious, it seems to me, that the material world is not a by-product of *human* minds. We do not create the universe. Some quantum physicists – John Wheeler, for example – have held that matter, in the form in which we perceive it, cannot exist without observing minds.[3] This view is based on experimental findings from such things as the delayed-choice double-slit experiment, which is alleged to show that probability-waves only collapse into particles ('matter') when they are observed or at least subjected by intelligent minds to measurement.[4] Wheeler at one point held

---

[3] John Wheeler writes, 'It has not really happened, it is not a phenomenon, until it is an observed phenomenon' (in 'The Past and the Delayed-Choice Double-Slit Experiment', *Mathematical Foundations of Quantum Theory*, ed. A. R. Marlow, Academic Press, 1978, p. 14).

[4] A readable account of this experiment is given in ch. 4 of *The Grand Design* by Stephen Hawking and Leonard Mlodinow (Bantam, 2011), ending with the astonishing observation that 'Our observations of its [the universe's] current state affect its past and determine the different histories of the universe.' However one interprets this, it certainly entails that observation actually determines the history of physical reality, and thus completely undermines a materialist interpretation of reality.

that such things as the Big Bang did not exist until some human minds thought about it. This is too much for most people, even quantum physicists, to accept. The Big Bang, or whatever reality it expresses, brings human minds into existence, and not the other way round. Even Bishop Berkeley, a so-called 'immaterialist', thought that there was some sort of reality other than human which produced human beings, though he argued that such a reality had to exist in the mind of God. Wheeler does not talk about God, but he is probably not thinking that there was nothing at all to the Big Bang before humans thought of it. He may have meant that the Big Bang as we observe or imagine it did not exist before human minds thought of it. Berkeley similarly wrote that the universe did not exist *as we observe it* until God created the sort of appearances that we observe.[5] That makes much more sense than the widespread popular view that Berkeley denied the existence of matter altogether. But Berkeley did say that since the reality we observe does not depend on human minds, and since there is no matter without observation, there must have been a cosmic mind which produced matter, and which presumably goes on doing so.

I have suggested that minds consist of streams of experience – sights, sounds, sensations, feelings, and thoughts – that can be at least partly directed by an agent which is aware of them, that decides which of them are good or worthwhile, that tries to make some of those good things real, and that can then enjoy them. Can such a mind possibly exist without having a body and a brain? One can, I think, imagine a stream of experiences which is directed by an

[5] Berkeley, *Three Dialogues between Hylas and Philonous*. In the third dialogue, when he is asked what is meant by 'creation', Philonous says, 'All objects are eternally known by God . . . but when things . . . are, by a decree of God, perceptible to creatures, then are they said to begin a relative existence, with respect to created minds.' This 'existence relative to created minds' must be an objective change in the nature of God's ideas. It is what brings the physical universe, as it is able to be perceived by humans, into being. This is not 'immaterialism' in the commonly accepted (and Kantian) interpretation.

agent towards a valuable goal, which the agent then enjoys. But this agent and this stream of experiences, as we imagine it, may have no physical body or brain. Of course the fact that I can imagine something does not entail that it exists, and I am not suggesting that humans are such beings. But unless there is some hidden fact I have missed, this does mean that such beings could possibly exist.

Try as I might, I can see no reason for thinking that a mind without a material body is impossible. There can be experiences without any material things – dreams are experiences of things that have no material existence. You might think that all experiences have to be of things that are material, that are in space and have mass. But that is not true. We experience thoughts and mathematical truths, and they are not in space. We experience feelings, and they are not in space.

We can experience thoughts which have no material objects (we can think of unicorns and dragons, for instance), and we can have mental images of such things too. So perhaps some mind could experience thoughts and images of things which have no material existence. We can even imagine a mind which experienced the thought of every possible state of affairs that could ever be. It could think of many universes which do not exist. Then it could decide which possible states were good and worthwhile. It could give some of these states material existence – in other words, it could create one or more universes. And it could then experience a material universe and enjoy it.

Such an ultimate reality is, or is very like, what has usually been called 'God'. Many scientists who speculate on philosophical questions agree that classical materialism – the view that reality consists of nothing but small massy particles bumping into one another in an absolute and unique space-time – is intellectually obsolete. Accounts of the universe now regularly involve notions such as that of manifold space-times; quantum realities that exist at a more ultimate level than, and are very different from, massy particles in one specific space; and informational codes that contain instructions for building complex integrated structures displaying new sorts of emergent properties.

What this suggests is that the nature of the reality investigated by physics and biology is much more complex and mysterious than some Newtonian materialists thought (though of course Newton himself was as far from being a materialist as one can get). In particular, the role that information plays in any account of the structure of our universe has come to take on a new importance in recent years.[6] Information is commonly conceived, in one main meaning, as a set of instructions which has been conceived by some mind in order to bring about some state of affairs. In modern science the notion is used more widely than this, but there is clearly a close connection between the idea of information and the idea of a mind which might conceive or understand and apply it. An analysis of the idea of information can therefore be quite revealing of what it would mean for the cosmos to be a creation of some quasi-mental reality.

Most theorists distinguish three main types of information: Shannon information, 'shaping' information, and semantic information. Shannon information is a matter of how to input the maximum amount of information into a closed physical system. It is concerned, it might be said, with quantity rather than quality, in that it totally ignores questions of the significance or function of the information that a physical system might contain. This is a technical matter for information technologists, and I shall not consider it further.

---

[6] See the collection of essays in *Information and the Nature of Reality*, ed. Paul Davies and Niels Gregersen (Cambridge University Press, 2010). Some of the material in the following sections of this chapter is found in a different version in my paper 'God as the Ultimate Informational Principle'.

'Shaping' or 'coding' information is the sort of thing we might have in mind when thinking of how DNA carries the information for constructing proteins and organic cells and bodies. We can understand what DNA is only when we see not only its chemical composition but also how that composition leads to the construction of bodies.

Few biologists, however, think that this function of DNA is actually designed, in the sense of being intentionally set up in order to achieve the purpose of building a body. DNA, it is very widely thought, has evolved by processes of random mutation and natural selection to be an efficient replicating mechanism. Even at this stage, it must be said that mutation is not 'random' in the sense that anything might happen. The mutations that occur, though they are certainly not all improvements, are such that some organisms do become more complex and better adapted to their environment. And the environment, at least on earth, is conducive to the development of complex integrated organisms that eventually generate conscious life. Perhaps the process is not quite so blind and undirected as some biologists suppose.[7]

Nevertheless, for many biologists the use of functional language is only necessary as a shortcut for understanding more basic chemical processes which are far too complex to be spelled out in detail. This is epistemological emergence with a reductionist ontology – the basic mechanisms are all ordinary chemical ones, but it is easier for us to understand them if we speak of functions and codes that can be 'read' and interpreted by ribosomes. We could reduce this language to that of chemistry, but it is too cumbersome to bother.

---

[7] Simon Conway Morris, in *Life's Solution* (Cambridge University Press, 2003), argues for convergence in evolution – that is, that certain paths through biological space are sooner or later bound to be taken, because of the nature of molecular bonding and of the environment. The evolutionary path is thus not wholly random but is very likely to end with the generation of intelligent life, by the ordinary mechanisms of physical nature.

A rather different, and I think more satisfactory, view is that we could not even in principle reduce the language of biology or psychology to that of chemistry or physics. Even though no new physical entities are involved, the way the basic physical entities interrelate and organise means that integrated and complex entities act in accordance with new principles, not ones deductively derivable from or reducible to those of their simpler physical constituents.[8]

So, for instance, the laws of nations are not reducible to laws governing the relation of all their constituent persons, but nations contain no entities but persons. It is their organisation into complex structures that produces new principles of interaction, though it produces no new physical entities (nations are not super-persons). Such new principles of interaction might be informational, in that some parts provide the information that governs the behaviour of other parts within the whole or that enables the whole to be constructed as a complex entity.

It seems as though the position of an entity within a structure, and the forms of its relation to other entities in that structure, calls forth new principles of interaction, causing it to function as part of a complex integrated totality.

New laws of nature, new ways of interaction, emerge that are not just reducible to the laws of interacting particles considered in isolation. Structure becomes important to understanding. Many informational systems may be understood as having a specific function within an integrated totality that emerges only when that totality exists as a system.

These facts have led some scientists to speak of holistic explanation – explanation of elementary parts in terms of a greater whole –

---

[8] This is the view of biologist Arthur Peacocke, as set out in *Creation and the World of Science* (Clarendon, 1979). While this view is sophisticated and complex, it does not quite seem to allow that conscious intelligence introduces new ontological factors (new 'entities') into reality, as well as new principles of organisation.

as an appropriate form of scientific explanation. Some, especially quantum physicists, extend the idea of holistic explanation to the whole universe, considered as a total physical system.

Recent hypotheses in quantum physics suggest that the whole physical universe is entangled in such a way that the parts of a system – even the behaviour of elementary particles – cannot be fully understood without seeing their role within a greater whole: ultimately the whole of space-time. The phenomenon of entanglement, or the non-local connection of subatomic particles, is well established. Since in the early stages of the development of the cosmos, when the cosmos was very small, virtually every particle that came into being would have interacted locally with other particles, it seems that in our presently expanded cosmos no limits can be placed on the possible non-local entanglement of the physical particles that it contains, however far away from one another they may now be.

Thus in our present cosmos there seem to be laws of interaction that can be fully specified only from a grasp of whole systems, rather than atomistically. In quantum cosmology we are encouraged to see the whole universe as a complex system and to think that knowledge of the total system may be needed fully to explain the behaviour of its simple parts.[9]

Perhaps the origin of the universe, the explanation of which is the elusive Holy Grail of cosmology, can be fully understood only when its fullest development is understood and we see its simplest and earliest parts as necessarily presupposed to the fully developed structure in which a consistent and rich set of its possibilities of interaction has been manifested. For a physics in which time is just one coordinate variable of what can in principle be considered a

---

[9] John Polkinghorne, in *Exploring Reality* (Yale University Press, 2005), p. 30ff., argues for this point of view.

totality, this is not too fantastic a notion. It might mean the return of final causality, in a new sense, to science. Only in the light of the manifestation of all the inherent possibilities of the universe, or at least of one set of compossible and extensive space-time states, might we be able to explain the properties of its originating simple parts.

We might think, as some quantum theorists do, of there being a set of possible states in phase space. The set of all possible states would form an archetype of the possibilities for a universe. Instead of a wholly arbitrary set of ultimate laws and states that proceeds by wholly random processes to an unanticipated outcome, we might have a set of possibilities from which one set of consistent laws might be actualised. This set might include this space-time as one of many actualised states, or it might be the only consistently actualisable universe that contains intelligent agents like us. Mathematical physicists have proposed both possibilities.

Why, after all, should we think that the earliest and the simplest could provide a complete explanation of the later and more complex? Perhaps that idea belongs to an outdated mechanistic physics for which time is an absolute mono-linear flow. Might we not think that the latest and most comprehensive state of a system, or the system taken as a whole, explains the simple origins? For the most comprehensive state would include the specification of many possible states and a selection of actual states in terms of value (value being a notion that can be filled out in various ways). Then the laws of nature would not be wholly arbitrary principles of interaction. They would be principles necessary to the fruition of a coherent, complex, organised, and integrated universe of unique and inexponable value.

We could then speak of a supreme informational principle of the universe as the mathematically richest and most fertile set of states in logical space that could give rise to a physical cosmos that could be valued for its own sake. A primordial set of mathematically possible states (a set that would exist necessarily and could not come into being or pass away) plus a selective principle of evaluation (a rule for ordering these states) would provide the informational code for constructing an actual universe.

That sense of information would be importantly different from the sense in which, for instance, DNA is a code for building bodies. It would precede, and not be the result of, any and all physical processes, evolutionary or otherwise. And it would not be part of the physical system for which it was a container and transmitter of information. But it would be analogous to shaping information, in that it would contain the patterns of all possible physical configurations and a principle of selecting between possibilities.

If we cast around for some model for a non-physical carrier of information containing patterns for possible existents, together with rules for ordering such patterns evaluatively, the historical example that springs to mind, or at least to the mind of any philosopher, is Plato's world of Forms. This is precisely a world of archetypes in which the phenomena of the physical cosmos participate partially and imperfectly.

In some modern science such a Platonic model has proved attractive to mathematicians, and Roger Penrose, for one, has said that the Platonic realm is for him more real than the physical realm. It has a mathematical purity, immutability, and necessity that the observable physical world lacks. 'To me', writes Penrose, 'the world of perfect forms is primary . . . its existence being almost a logical necessity – and . . . the world of conscious perceptions and the world of physical reality are its shadows.'[10]

Plato had difficulty in relating the world of Forms (of possible states in phase space) to a dynamic power that could translate it into

[10] Roger Penrose, *Shadows of the Mind* (Oxford University Press, 1994), p. 417.

an actual physical embodiment. It might be said that Stephen Hawking had a similar difficulty when he asked, in *A Brief History of Time*, 'What is it that breathes fire into the equations and makes a universe for them to describe?'[11] How could a set of mathematical principles, however elegant and necessary they might be, give rise to a physical cosmos? In Plato's dialogue *Timaeus*, the Demiurge, or world architect, uses the Forms as models for constructing a universe but seems strangely disconnected from the Forms themselves.[12] It was Augustine, in the Christian tradition, who formed the elegant postulate that the Forms were actually in the mind of God, necessary components of the divine being, which was the actual basis of their otherwise merely possible reality.[13] Thus the concepts of information, integrated complexity, and holistic explanation can lead to the idea of an ultimate cosmic mind.

[11] Stephen Hawking, *A Brief History of Time* (Bantam, 1988), ch. 12.   [12] Plato, *Timaeus*, 29d–30d.
[13] See Augustine, *De Trinitate*, book 8, ch. 2.

CHAPTER 9

The Supreme Informational Principle

With the introduction of the idea of mind or consciousness as the carrier of possibilities, there is some motivation to move beyond the view that higher-level laws are just shorthand substitutes for boringly laborious lists of lower-level laws, as well as beyond the view that they are new principles of interaction between complex systems, the basic nature of the elements of such systems remaining what it always was. We may have to introduce the idea of consciousness as a distinctive kind of existent.

Consciousness is not just a new form of relationship between complex physical systems. Apprehension and understanding, and intelligent action for the sake of realising some envisaged but not yet existent goal, are properties not of physically measurable entities but of a distinctive sort of reality that is not material.

If we posit consciousness as a distinctive kind of existent, we move to the third use of the term *information* – the semantic use, when some physical item (a written mark or sound) provides information about something other than itself to some consciousness that understands it. There are three main components here: (1) the physical item, (2) the person who takes it to refer or to indicate that some operation is to be carried out, and (3) what it is about or (in logic and mathematics, for example) the operation it instructs one to perform.

Digital computers operate in accordance with the second type of information. The computer is structured so that some of its physical components constitute a code for performing operations – there are physical elements with a function. But there is no one who understands the instructions; they operate automatically. Of course computer codes have been intentionally structured precisely so that the codes can be used for specific purposes and the results on the screen can be understood by someone. That is the whole point of having computers. They are designed to help persons understand things, and they provide information only when someone does understand what they produce.

Without that act of understanding, there is no information. There is only the material substratum that stores information – but that material basis needs to be interpreted by an act of intellectual understanding to become actual information. This is the point made by John Searle's 'Chinese Room' thought experiment.[1] A person who does not understand Chinese can nevertheless respond to Chinese symbols passed to her through a grill. With the aid of a library of characters, they can find appropriate responses to those symbols. But she does not understand either the messages or the responses. There has been much debate about Searle's example, but I think it is a picturesque way of putting a point that I strongly agree with – semantic information requires something more than computation. The material substratum needs to be interpreted by an act of intellectual understanding to become actual information.

That is why the information carried by DNA molecules is not information in the semantic sense. The code does provide a programme for constructing an organism, but no finite person has constructed it and no consciousness needs to understand and apply the programme. It has originated by ordinary evolutionary processes, and, like a computer programme, it operates without the need for conscious interpretation.

[1] John Searle, 'Minds, Brains, and Programs', in *Behavioural and Brain Sciences* 3, 1980.

Nevertheless, there may be a holistic explanation for the general process of evolution and for the sorts of organisms that DNA codes construct. If we are looking for a total system within which random (i.e. not specifically directed in every case in order to achieve some beneficial consequence) mutations and natural selection of specific kinds of organisms occur, we might find in the ecosystem itself and its history a recipe for the generation of more complex physical systems and for the gradual development of organisms capable of conscious apprehension and creative response. Paul Davies and Simon Conway Morris are just two of the scientists who see in the basic physical foundations of the evolutionary process a vector to the virtually inevitable development of conscious and responsive life.[2]

It is extraordinary that a physical system generates informational codes for constructing complex integrated organisms. But that fact does not of itself require the introduction of any external designing intelligence. What is more extraordinary is that these organisms then generate a quite new sort of information – semantic information – that does involve consciousness, interpretation, intention, and understanding.

In my view, such things as conscious intention and understanding have real existential status. They are irreducible and distinctive forms of reality. They are kinds of stuff that are not reducible to the properties of physical elements such as electrons. Yet they come into existence at the end of a many-billion-year-long process of development from simple physical elements.

If we are not simply to give up all attempts at explanation and say that consciousness is just a random by-product of the evolutionary process, we must look for a different type of explanation. This is

[2] See Simon Conway Morris, *Life's Solution* (Cambridge University Press, 2003), and Paul Davies, *The Mind of God* (Simon and Schuster, 1992).

one to which contemporary biologists have largely been temperamentally averse but which is now increasingly being forced upon our attention – that is, a cosmic, holistic explanation in which the development of the parts is explained by their contribution to the existence of an integrated totality giving rise to emergent consciousnesses.

The ideas of holism and emergence suggest the synthesising idea of a primordial consciousness that is ontologically prior to all physical realities, that contains the coded information for constructing any possible universe, and that produces emergent realities which can contribute to the sorts of value for the sake of which one possible universe may exist. This would certainly provide a strong reason for the existence of a universe containing finite consciousnesses that could share in appreciating, and even in creating, some of the distinctive values potential in the basic structure of the universe: for such a creation would increase the total amount and the kinds of value in existence. One reason for the existence of a physical cosmos is that it is generated by a primordial consciousness as a condition of the possibility of communities of multiple self-developing finite minds. They in turn make possible the existence of new kinds of values which otherwise could not exist.

Whether or not one calls such a primordial consciousness 'God' is partly a matter of taste. For some – including probably both Hawking and Einstein – the idea of God is too anthropomorphic, too primitive and sentimental, to be of use. But if some notion of value is introduced, as a reason for actualising some rather than other logically possible states, the notion of consciousness seems to be implied. For it is consciousness that apprehends and appreciates value. Only intelligent consciousness can have a reason for bringing about some state, and that reason would precisely be the actualisation and appreciation of some as yet merely possible value.

Consciousness, as a distinctive sort of real existent not composed of purely physical elements has been a major problem for classical materialism, and implausible attempts have even been made to deny that it exists at all. But quantum physics throws doubt on such denials. When quantum physics speaks of the collapse of a wave function when an observation is made, some quantum physicists – I have already mentioned John Wheeler – hold that consciousness is involved in the actualisation of possibilities in a constitutive way.

So for some physicists (and the list would be long, including Wheeler, Henry Stapp, Eugene Wigner, John von Neumann, and Bernard D'Espagnat) consciousness is involved in the very existence of physical nature as it appears to us. Consciousness as we know it is capable of conceiving possibilities as well as apprehending actualities, and of making possibilities actual for a reason. Thus a hypothesis consonant with many interpretations of quantum physics is to see the actual world as rooted in a consciousness that conceives all possible states and actualises some of them for a reason connected with the evaluation of such states by that consciousness.

Such a reason might be that only one set of compossible states gives rise to a complex, interesting, and enduring universe – Leibniz's hypothesis.[3] Or it may be that any universe can be actualised that exhibits a unique set of valued states, in which the values markedly outweigh the disvalues and the disvalues are compensated in a way ultimately acceptable to those who have experienced them – Aquinas' hypothesis.[4]

Rather as DNA may be seen as an informational code for constructing organisms, so the basic laws of physics – the laws of the interaction of complex as well as simple physical systems – can be

---

[3] Leibniz, *Monadology*, 1714, paras. 53–55.
[4] Aquinas, *Summa Theologiae*, 1a, question 23, article 6.

seen as informational codes for developing societies of conscious intelligent agents out of simpler physical elements.

However, the laws of physics did not, like DNA, evolve by mutation and selection, and they are not embodied in chemical or physical elements. Even those, like Lee Smolin, who speak of an evolution of physical laws have to presuppose a prior set of laws that can account for such evolution. As a matter of logic, the laws in accordance with which physical entities relate cannot be generated by the relations between such entities. At least some basic set of laws must be seen as primordial and constitutive of reality rather than emergent from it.

My suggestion (it is actually the suggestion of many classical philosophers and theologians, and a suggestion that much modern physics supports rather than undermines) is that such basic laws can be fully understood only when they themselves are seen as preconditions for developing consciousness and intelligence from simple physical elements.

But then we have to see such conscious intelligence as a primary causal factor in the generation and nature of those simple physical elements. To adapt John Wheeler's suggestion a little, the simple originating phenomena of the universe may not even exist unless they are conceived, evaluated, and intentionally actualised by consciousness.

For some physicists, and I think for Wheeler, it is the final conscious state of the universe itself that is a causal factor in its own physical origin. The universe generates a cosmic intelligence that then becomes cause of its own originating processes. But what this paradoxical suggestion really points to is the existence of a trans-temporal consciousness that can originate the universe as a condition of the existence of the sorts of consciousnesses the universe generates through and in time.

CHAPTER 10

Explaining the Universe

It has been objected, most publicly by Richard Dawkins in recent times,[1] that a primordial cosmic consciousness is just too complex a thing to be likely to exist. The simple is more likely to exist than the complex, he says, and so to appeal to a cosmic consciousness is to try to explain the improbable in terms of the even more improbable – and that can hardly count as an explanation.

One may suspect, however, that something has gone wrong here with the use of the idea of probability. It is false that the simple is more likely to exist than the complex; there are infinitely more complex possible states than simple states, and so, on a simple view of probability as a function of the number of alternative states that could exist, a complex state is more likely to exist than a simple one. But of course no single possible state is either more or less likely to exist than any other possible state. Probability does not really work when considering the likelihood of anything at all existing when there is nothing in existence to compare that thing with. Considerations of probability alone cannot tell us what is likely to exist out of the complete array of all possible states of affairs. So a cosmic consciousness is not in fact any more improbable than the allegedly very simple and purely physical initial state of the universe.

---

[1] Richard Dawkins, *The God Delusion* (Bantam, 2006).

It may seem rather odd, however, to think of a 'complete array of all possible states'. In what sense would such a thing exist? Things, it may be said, are either actual or non-existent; there cannot be actually existent possibles. To put the point as Aquinas did, actuality is prior to possibility,[2] and possibilities cannot exist unless they exist in something actual. One example of the way possibilities may exist is the way in which people may conceive of possible states, but only if they have actual minds which do the conceiving.

Many scientists, including Einstein, have thought that the cosmos could be adequately explained if we could root it in something which exists by necessity.[3] Then we would no longer be able to ask why things are as they are, since we would see that they could not be otherwise and since nothing could either cause them or destroy them. The laws of mathematics or physics might turn out to be necessarily what they are, and they might somehow necessarily generate a physical cosmos. So the laws of physics might take the place of God or consciousness as the ultimate reality.[4]

This thought is appealing with regard to mathematics, where things could not be any different than they are and mathematical truths are not brought to be or destroyed in time. It is rather less appealing in physics, since physical laws could be different and laws do not seem like the sorts of things that could generate a cosmos, or indeed that could generate anything at all.

[2] Aquinas, *Summa Theologiae*, 1a, question 3, article 1.
[3] Einstein wrote, 'The enterprise of physics is ... to reach as far as possible the utopian and seemingly arrogant aim of knowing why nature is thus and not otherwise ... thereby one experiences, so to speak, that God himself could not have arranged these connections in any other way' (*Festschrift for Aunel Stadola*, Orell Fussli, 1929), p. 126.
[4] Stephen Hawking canvasses this possibility in *The Grand Design* when he says, 'Because there is a law like gravity, the universe can and will create itself from nothing ... [I]t is not necessary to invoke God to light the blue touch paper and set the universe going' (p. 227). This quotation contradicts the passage I have cited in Chapter 8, note 4, where he makes consciousness much more important to fundamental reality than this.

Even in mathematics, equations do not just lie around like rocks in a landscape. Equations are more like operational principles of structure, order, and relationship. It is minds which conceive and understand equations. And mathematicians operate with equations with an aim in mind. Mathematicians aim at elegance and beauty and formal simplicity, and there is a great aesthetic pleasure in constructing an elegant formalism. The intrinsic value of a great mathematical proof is probably not appreciated by a great number of people, but it exists all the same. It is perceived by those who have the ability to carry out the intellectual operations that enable them to appreciate the proof.

The laws of physics, which usually take a mathematical form, also seem to be formal operating principles for possible physical structures. They are not purely descriptive of actual worlds, but they describe the structures of possible worlds (in quantum cosmology, apparently already existing laws govern the sorts of universes that can come into being). It is minds which conceive of possible worlds, and at least some of these (like a 'world' of mathematical theorems or basic moral axioms) are necessarily what they are. A mind which conceives of and contains or 'generates' necessary truths must itself be necessary, at least in some respects (obviously including the respects in which it generates necessary truths). So the primordial mind which is the container of necessary truths is a necessary mind – a mind which, in some respects, has to exist with just the changeless nature that it has. It will be constituted in part by the complete array of all possible states.

A common way of thinking of a complete array of all possible states is to think of them as simultaneously present in detail, fully specified. Any created and contingent future would have to consist in the selection of some of these possible states. In a sense, there would never be anything that was radically new and that had not already existed, as a possibility, in the mind of God. But once we have introduced the idea of mind as the container of possibilities, there is an alternative conception.

A truly creative mind could perhaps generate radically new possibilities (which would not exist even as possibilities before they were conceived). For such a mind, some possibilities could be generated by imaginative mental activity. We might think, by analogy, of the activity of a creative human mind; for instance, think of Mozart writing a new symphony. There would exist an array of possible states (the notes). There would exist a set of rules for combining those states (the rules of harmony). Working with those states and rules, Mozart can compose a new work that perhaps did not previously exist as a complete possibility even in the mind of God. Genuine creativity might thereby have a place in the universe.

If we now think of the cosmos itself, we may suppose that there will be a primordially existent set of possible states laying down general patterns not specified in exhaustive detail for sorts of universes that may exist. There will similarly be a set of possible rules (various possible laws of nature) which will govern interactions between those states. There will also be a set of ideal, intrinsically worthwhile goals which could be realised in various possible universes. These primordial patterns, rules, and ideal goals will presumably be necessary features of the divine life. They will constitute the set of primordial possibilities in the mind of God.

In addition to those primordial possibilities, however, there may be scope for truly creative and radically new decisions about what specific and fully specified possibilities will be realised in a given universe. Such creative decisions might be made by the cosmic mind itself, which would thereby be contingent in respect to those decisions, although necessary in respect to the primordial array of possibilities. Or some creative decisions might be made by other created minds which are emergent societies within a web or communion of intelligent finite agents.

The cosmic mind would be necessary in the sense that some of its contents – and therefore its existence as a reality that necessarily contains such contents and necessarily has the capacity to generate new contents – could not be other than it is in its general nature. It would also, as a matter of necessity, be contingent in some respects, having the capacity to make new creative decisions with regard to the existence of specific universes and events within them. The reality and general nature of such a mind, being necessary, cannot be brought into being, destroyed, or changed by addition or subtraction. It would not make sense to ask what caused it, for it is the condition of any causes existing. It would not make sense to ask why it is the way it is, for it includes every possibility within itself, and so there is no alternative that it does not already include or have, uniquely, the capacity to generate.

The point about such a cosmic consciousness is that it is not supposed to exist with a certain degree of probability. It is supposed to exist necessarily. It is something that could not fail to exist, if there is to be such a thing as an actual array of possible states. Some think that the fact that anything exists is ultimately just a brute fact for which there can be no explanation.[5] But this may not be so. I think it makes sense to say that there is some being that exists necessarily. That is, it exists in every possible world, for it is the

---

[5] Richard Swinburne seems to hold such a view – see *The Coherence of Theism* (Oxford University Press, 1977), part 3. I argue for a stronger sense of necessity than Swinburne does, a sense in which God cannot fail to exist with the basic nature that God has. This seems to me a coherent notion to which sense can be given by postulating that 'the mind which conceives of every possible state' exists in every possible world – which seems obviously true of the idea of God, though it is not, as Anselm thought, a proof that God must exist.

actual basis of any and all possible worlds, and consequently of every actual world too.[6] Its nature is no doubt extremely mysterious and unpicturable. But if we are to seek for some remote analogy, it is most like what we know of as mind.

Some laws or principles could also be necessary in the sense that they are conditions of (necessary to) realising a set of distinctive values (reasonable goals of action). Those values in turn would be necessarily what they are if there is an array of possible states that can generally be ranked in order of value. So if we can think of an array of possible states, with the values they necessarily have, there would be an intrinsic reason for the existence of any universe – namely, the goodness that it would exhibit. For to say that something is intrinsically worthwhile is to give a wholly satisfactory (though axiological, evaluational, and not scientific) explanation for its existence.

We are operating at a level of great abstraction here, but my main point can be made simply. If there is no ultimate reason for anything existing, then it is not true that the simple is more likely to exist than the complex. But if there is an ultimate reason for the universe, if the universe is ultimately rational, the reason would have to lie in the goodness or intrinsic value of certain possible states that is necessarily what it is.

The trouble with Professor Hawking's idea of laws that are necessary in themselves, and need no God 'to light the blue touch paper and set the universe going', is that no idea is given of how

[6] Alvin Plantinga has undertaken an analysis of the idea of necessary existence in *The Nature of Necessity* (Oxford University Press, 1974), and he argues that it is logically possible that there could be a being which exists in every possible world. This being would then exist necessarily. If one argues that one can imagine a possible world without this being, the response would be that one has simply not considered the conditions under which possibilities can be said to exist (they must exist in something actual, and this may be the same thing in all possible worlds). I do not think, as Plantinga then did, that this proves that there is one and only one necessary being. But I do think it proves that such a being is possible, as far as we can tell. And that at least shows that it is an option for thought, which may be part of a general conceptual framework for explaining the existence of the universe.

laws – principles of logical operation – could exist without some intellectual power to conceive them, with no causal power to act on them, and with no notion of their relative values which could provide a principle of selection between different possible laws. Such a hypothesis therefore both fails to account for many perceived features of our cosmos – those especially involving intelligent consciousness and normative notions of truth, beauty, and goodness – and fails to provide a convincing reason for the selection of one possible cosmos out of many others. The postulation of a mind-like reality that could conceive, select, and implement laws seems to me to have greater explanatory force.

What I have presented is, and is meant to be, a basically Platonic idea – an idea that has been revived in recent years by, among others, John Leslie[7] and Roger Penrose.[8] I have suggested, following Augustine, that mind or consciousness is somehow involved in such an ultimate explanation, because it is mind that stores possibilities non-physically and mind that can act for a reason – that is, in order to make actual some such possible states. This is just to say that mind is a fundamental constituent of ultimate reality and is necessarily prior to all physical entities. For they are actualisations of possibilities apprehended by cosmic mind, the only actuality that is not capable of being brought into being or of not existing or of being other than it is, precisely because it is a condition of the existence of any possibilities whatsoever. Cosmic consciousness is the condition of any and all possibilities existing (and at least some possibilities necessarily do), and not merely a very complex thing that just happens to exist.

In this and Chapters 8 and 9, two types of information have been discussed: shaping information and semantic information. For the

---

[7] John Leslie, *Universes* (Routledge, 1989).
[8] Roger Penrose, *Shadows of the Mind* (Oxford University Press, 1994).

former, information is a code for the construction of complex integrated systems and is best understood by holistic explanation. This suggests, though it does not entail, a holistic (whole part), emergent (progressively developing new properties), axiological (value-oriented), and purposive view of the cosmic order which is definitely non-materialistic but leaves the question of the ultimate basis of such value-directed order unresolved.

For the latter, information needs to be understood and intentionally communicated by intelligent consciousnesses. Humans are such consciousnesses, and they are integral parts of a cosmos which moves towards the emergence of finite conscious states that are of intrinsic value. Humans stand in a continuum that begins from the much simpler capacity of physical objects to respond to stimuli from an environment of other objects. The registration of the stimulus, the largely automatic response, and the form of interaction with other objects are elementary forms of what becomes, in humans, conscious apprehension, creative response, and personal relationships with other persons.

Even the simplest physical object registers information from its environment, interprets it, and acts on the basis of it – but of course none of these simple capacities involves consciousness or awareness. There is nothing there that is truly creative, and there is no development, as there is with human persons, of a unique historical trajectory, no sense of an inward spiritual journey or a novel and unpredictable history.

As organisms become more complex and integrated, these primitive capacities of registration and response are extended and become more diverse and individual. Consciousness seems to be a continuously emergent property that is so closely integrated with organic systems that it may seem right to call it an emergent aspect of a monistic and naturalistic system. The aspects of conscious experience and brain activity can, however improperly in the case of humans, be torn apart. So it is possible to have a consciousness without a body – God is such – and it is possible to have a functioning brain without consciousness (although we assume that this does not normally, or perhaps ever, happen). Humans are fully embodied minds. Yet in human consciousness an important threshold is crossed to full semantic information, and that suggests the idea of ultimate reality as a consciousness that holds the information necessary to create any universe, the ultimate ontological and informational principle.

Such a principle would be logically prior to and ontologically different from any actual physical state. A Platonic-Augustinian model for such a principle is the world of Forms, an ultimate informational system carried and transmitted by a cosmic mind. This is a fully semantic sense of information for which data are understood and interpreted as significant by consciousness. It carries complete information about all possible states in phase-space, states that carry necessary evaluative rankings and thus provide an internal reason for the existence of one or more actual universes. This would provide an ultimate axiological explanation for the existence of our universe. This is the mind of God.

Of course this rather abstract idea of God is not all that Christians think of as God. It is more like the 'God of the philosophers and scientists' of which Pascal complained (in the 'Memorial' found after his death, sewn into his clothing). But it is important to show that the idea of a supreme mind which brings about the universe is a possible and reasonable idea. There is much more to learn about God, and we might expect that if there was such a supreme mind, it would have brought about the universe for a good reason. It is therefore natural to think that in some way it would reveal what that reason was. Christians believe that this is what is revealed in and through the person of Jesus Christ. Perhaps we need to think that there could well be a God, and that the idea of God is a natural and rational one, before we can take Jesus' life and teaching seriously. No one who has studied the history of philosophy will expect all philosophers to agree with one another. But I think that at least we should allow that belief in God is firmly grounded in hard philosophical thinking about the bases of human knowledge. It is not just a piece of blind and irrational imagination.

It also has very real practical consequences. If the universe is a product of mind, then it obviously exists for a purpose. It has a goal, and the goal will be realised. It is not just an accident, without any purpose at all. Furthermore, the purpose will be good, because minds choose things because they think those things are good or worthwhile. If the universe is a product of mind, it will therefore have been chosen precisely in order to realise worthwhile states. And we humans will have a part to play in that purpose, since we have been chosen to exist as well. It seems likely that each human person will have a personal moral goal, and that goal will be part of the moral purpose of the universe as a whole. That is a completely different perspective on life from thinking that we are accidental by-products of a blind and indifferent universe. It may have huge practical consequences for the ways in which humans live and see the purpose of their lives.

Creation and Evolution

A supreme creative mind is possible. I suggest that it is much more plausible than the main competing theory that human minds just originate from matter, without any design or purpose. The reason is that matter does not need minds, and indeed in a totally materialist universe minds are a totally unexpected by-product of matter, and they will be eliminated anyway as the physical universe decays. But in an idealist universe finite minds need something like matter, at least if there are to be many minds which gain new information and interact with one another. For human minds gain their information from a shared environment. They recognise one another by the observable bodies that they have. And they act in an environment which gives them the capacities and physical powers that they have. So if mind is the ultimate reality, there is a good reason why it should give rise to a material universe.

The supreme Creative Mind does not need anything like matter in this way, because it gains its information from thought, not matter; because it does not interact with other minds of the same sort (there is only one creator); and because it does not have a body or act in a material world. In this sense, primordial mind is complete and all-sufficient in itself.

However, if the Creator generates a material world, then finite minds can emerge from that world, and the Creator can know and interact with them in new ways. Creativity and personal relationship are good things. If they are to exist, then the supreme mind must create a universe in which new things happen and from which many finite persons can emerge. Thus the Creator has a good reason to create a material world and to create finite minds as well. Indeed, it seems that such creation would be an expression of the nature of the Creator. But this means that the material world must have exactly the sort of properties that are needed so that minds can emerge from matter, in a new but natural way. And the amazing thing is that it does.[1] In this way, the picture of one supreme mind creating matter so that other minds can emerge by natural processes seems to be much more plausible than the picture of minds springing into existence for no reason, quite unexpectedly, and having no purpose or point at all.

This means that there is a good reason why the universe exists and why we exist. It means that the Creator values the world and values us. Thus it is right for us to value the beauty of the created universe, attempt to appreciate and understand it deeply and fully, and care for it and seek to realise its inherent possibilities for good. In the present age, when we have the power to destroy our planet, we have a special responsibility to respect and preserve the beauty and variety of our world.

In addition, Christians have a special reason to value the material universe, because they believe that the Creator took human form and united human nature to the divine nature in Jesus. Thus the natural world has been sanctified, united to God, and in this way given a sort of sacred nature. Nature might not be divine, but in Christ it has been united to the divine. This means that we must be especially sensitive to even quite ordinary material things, since

---

[1] Stephen Hawking writes, 'The laws of nature form a system that is extremely fine-tuned, and very little in physical law can be altered without destroying the possibility of the development of life as we know it' (*The Grand Design*, p. 205).

they too have a share in and in some way express the divine nature. Christians do not worship nature, but insofar as it can be united to God they must respect, love, and care for nature.

There is, however, a problem with this account. The story that evolution has to tell – at least as it is often told – is of a ruthless competition for survival in which a constant battle against rivals is necessary for existence. T. H. Huxley, in a famous lecture on 'Evolution and Ethics',[2] held that we have no moral lessons to learn from nature and indeed are bound to oppose nature's insensitivity to all the particular forms of life which it indiscriminately and inconsiderately spews forth. This hardly seems like unalloyed respect, love, and care.

This evolutionary story has been examined theologically many times, and I do not want to do much more here than remark that a theist cannot accept that the process is blind, accidental, or morally unjustifiable. However the world is, God is its ultimate source and has for it a purpose which is good. It is difficult now to say, as it has often in the past been said in the Christian tradition, that at some time in the past nature was perfect but became corrupted as a result of human sin. We now know that suffering and death have been parts of the evolutionary story since long before human life existed, and if destruction and pain are ever to be abolished from nature, it will be in the future and as a result of human effort. We might not be very optimistic about this possibility, but it does mean a change in orientation from looking sadly to lost perfection towards looking hopefully to future perfectibility.

Christians are committed to thinking that the whole universe is created by a good God for a purpose, and the cosmic optimism that things might get better is rooted originally in the Jewish prophetic

---

[2] T. H. Huxley, *Evolution and Ethics* (Pilot Press, 1947).

hope for the coming of a society of justice and love, and for a renewed creation – so clearly adumbrated in the Old Testament book of the prophet Isaiah. Christians tend to have a darker and more pessimistic view of the possibility of this society within the historical process. They still, however, look for a realisation of the frustrated potentialities of this world in a renewed creation, perhaps at the end of historical time. Several important passages in the New Testament stress that salvation is not a matter of humans being taken out of the realm of nature into a different, heavenly world, leaving this cosmos to decay. God's purpose is in Christ 'to reconcile to himself all things, whether on earth or in heaven' (Colossians 1, 19). The same theme is found in Ephesians, where God's plan is said to be to 'unite all things in him [Christ], all things in heaven and things on earth' (Ephesians, 1, 9). It is the whole creation which groans in travail, waiting for redemption, and God's plan is to create a new heaven and earth, which will be this universe transformed, not simply somewhere quite different.

On this view, the universe is acknowledged to be imperfect and alienated from God in some way. But its destiny is to be united in and reconciled to God. Christ's work is not concerned only with saving human souls. It is concerned with renewing the whole of nature. Nature is to be brought to its proper perfection through the work of those who are filled with the Spirit of Christ. It follows that we must respect the earth as owned and loved by God, as suffering to a great extent from human alienation from God, as waiting for redemption, and as calling for human responsible action to liberate it from frustration and bring it to its intended fulfilment.

All this is predicated on the thought that there is a purpose in the cosmic process. Many biologists would reject that view, but there is nothing that contradicts the findings of the biological sciences in the view that there is an inborn propensity in the natural order to the development of complex integrated intelligent life forms. The process by which the flickering and transient energies within the atom give rise to stable atomic compounds, then to self-replicating molecules of immense and integrated complexity, to the formation of central nervous systems which enable organisms to react consciously to their environment, and finally (on this planet at least) the emergence of the neocortex, making possible abstract understanding and responsible freedom, is readily interpretable as directed towards the genesis of intelligent life.[3] A creator who wishes intelligent life to be formed by such a process could well have set up the process so that it would sooner or later result in such intelligent life. I think those who believe that there is a creator are committed to viewing the process as purposive in this sense.

It does not follow that every detail of the process, as we now know it to be, is personally designed by a loving God. There have been so many blind alleys in evolution, and so many genetic mutations which have not proved conducive to survival, and so many dispositions built up over millennia which are now counter-productive to the sustenance of life that it is unconvincing to take nature, as William Paley did, as the perfect contrivance of a God who designs every detail for the best. That is not the only model of a purposive process. If a process is to culminate in societies of relational entities which have creative freedom and moral responsibility, then that process must allow for open social interaction, rational choice, and a degree of autonomous self-organisation. Even at its inception such a process cannot be a closed and universally deterministic one, or one that strictly proportions activity according to merit, or one in which everything

---

[3] Arthur Peacocke, in *Paths from Science towards God* (Oneworld Press, 2001), writes that the evolutionary process is one of 'unfolding the divinely endowed potentialities of the universe through a process in which its creative possibilities and propensities become actualised'.

always happens for the best. A closed deterministic system would render free choice impossible. A wholly just system would make it impossible for the violent to inflict harm on the innocent, and thus would render free social interaction impossible. A system in which everything happens for the best would make it impossible for irrational or vicious actions to occur, and so again render moral freedom impossible. What is needed is a mixture of law-like necessities, to make predictable actions possible, and of multiply related open sequences of events, to enable free creativity and relationship to emerge as natural consequences of the total system. The process would be a mixture of necessity, chance, competition, and creative purpose. Within it, not every entity would be striving to change or mutate, for it would be necessary for many entities to remain in a stable and simple state, as a foundation for more complex entities to build on. So the 'evolution' might consist in the occurrence and selection of a few mutations from a much wider array of some more and less stable entities. This fits a generally Darwinian picture of a few 'progressive' mutations within a much wider population in each generation, with a selection of the best adapted. It is consistent with a divinely ordered process aimed, in general, at the emergence of intelligent life forms, though the process would be constrained by necessities inherent in the system.[4]

I find such an evolutionary picture helpful in explaining the present condition of human nature as a complex mixture of altruism and egoism. But even if that picture is accepted, the problem of suffering, particularly animal suffering, in a God-created world remains. The evolutionary biologist Stephen J. Gould says, 'We need only think of the ugliness of *Sacculina* or a bladder worm, the

---

[4] Dr. Peacocke writes that God 'is an Improviser of unsurpassed ingenuity', setting up a system in which 'the full gamut of the potentialities of living matter could be explored'.

stupidity of a rhinoceros or a stegosaur, the horror of a female mantis devouring its mate, or a brood of ichneumon flies slowly eating out a caterpillar.'[5]

This is a strangely anthropomorphic view of nature. There is plenty of beauty in the molecular structure of a bladder worm, plenty of wisdom in the moulding of millions of electrons into a rhinoceros, and plenty of goodness in a system which brings intelligence out of the same natural processes which generate flies and caterpillars – organisms which, having no anterior cingulate or neocortex, do not feel pain in the way humans do. Nevertheless, there is enough pain and frustration in nature, even if only in conscious animals, to lead us to say that such things arise by necessities inherent in the physical structure of the cosmos, and not by a specific and freely chosen divine intention. The system and its goals may be divinely intended, but many specific features of the system exist by necessity, by chance, or by free finite choices, as unpreventable conditions or consequences of the system as a whole.

With regard to evolution, I would expect Christians to reject an interpretation of natural selection which is such that it is a matter of sheer chance which organisms survive – the Stephen Gould idea that if we ran the process of evolution on earth again, we would probably get a quite different result. There is little difficulty in rejecting such an interpretation, since if most of what happens does so as a result of the operation of laws of nature, then the author of those laws can know and ensure what the overall result of natural selection will be. The process can be set up to ensure the eventual genesis of rational sentient organisms, even specifically of human beings, if the conditions (the genetic and epigenetic landscapes) are

[5] Stephen J. Gould, 'Non-Moral Nature', in *The Sacred Beetle*, ed. M. Gardner (Oxford University Press, 1985).

specified closely enough.[6] In that sense, one can speak of a purpose in nature – a goal intended by God which nature's laws will realise in time.

This account of purpose in nature suggests four fundamental theological truths. First, the Christian ethical tradition of Natural Law is based on the premiss that one should not frustrate God's purpose. But if God's purpose is the genesis of rational sentient life and if many specific features of nature, like disease and natural disaster, themselves frustrate that purpose, it may become an obligation to 'interfere' with natural processes – as we do in modern medicine. It becomes a human obligation to cooperate with the divine purpose of enabling personal life to flourish by frustrating some of the natural biological processes which themselves impede that divine purpose. This does not resolve all the difficult ethical problems about human intervention to 'improve' nature. But it does provide an indication that not every natural process is in order as it is and that physical and biological processes must in the end be judged by their efficacy in promoting and preserving personal well-being – not, of course, of a privileged few, but of all personal beings. We might better speak of the general purposes of God in nature than of the purposes of nature itself.

Nature exists in order to realise definite values – values of love, creativity, and wisdom. The human species is the only one we know to be capable of morally responsible conduct, imaginative creativity, and intellectual comprehension – though there is no reason why other forms of beings should not be capable of them in other forms or on other planets, for example. We might say that it is not the human species which is important, but the values of responsible creative, intellectual, and social action, in whatever

[6] See Simon Conway Morris, *Life's Solution* (Cambridge University Press, 2003).

species such values may be realised. Any such beings – call them persons – would be made in the image of God, and nature exists in order that such beings should exist and flourish.

Second, nature is the stuff out of which such persons are formed. In contrast to some views according to which humans are spiritual souls trapped temporarily in matter, from which they hope one day to escape, the Biblical picture is that humans are formed from dust. Humans are not alien intrusions into the material; they are material. So humans are essentially parts of nature, their bodies made of the same atoms that every other physical object is made of. There is no basic contrast between persons and nature, since humans are parts of nature which have become persons. They are nature personalised.

Third, nature forms the environment within which persons exist, which is the proper object of contemplation and delight. Just as it dishonours other persons to treat them merely as objects to be used, manipulated, or cast aside, so it dishonours nature to treat it merely as an object to be used, manipulated, or destroyed. God delights in the beauty of the natural world (Proverbs 8, 22–31). In the billions of years before humans existed, the world was appreciated and valued by God. When humans come to exist, they can enter into this appreciation and valuing. Humans do not give nature its value; they come to share in a valuing which has existed as long as God has existed.

Fourth, nature can be a sacrament, in the wide sense of a physical expression of a spiritual presence. In the beauty of mountains and forests, desert and sea, there exists a physical expression of one part of the infinite being of God. As Schleiermacher put it, to see the infinite in the finite is true piety, and nature is the medium through which infinity can be manifested in some of its myriad forms. The proper human attitude to nature should therefore be one of reverence and appreciation. It is valued not only because God values it and takes delight in it, but also because it can mediate the presence of God.

This compels us to say that nature does not just exist instrumentally, as a means for bringing persons into existence. It has an intrinsic value of its own: as a sacrament of the divine presence, as an object of contemplation and delight, and as the widest boundary of the personal self, helping constitute personhood and make personhood what it is, not only as some sort of alien entity to which souls are temporarily attached.

CHAPTER 12

Is Nature Sacred?

The belief that nature has an intrinsic value of its own is the central moral point which is made by those who promote what is known as 'deep ecology'. The term was first used by the environmental philosopher Arne Naess, in an attempt to counter the widespread view that nature only has instrumental value. He says, 'The ecological self of a person is that with which this person identified.'[1] The hopeless egoist identifies with just one body and complex of feelings and thoughts. The tribalist identifies with a particular social group – it might well be Manchester United – which gives meaning and identity. Humanists embrace the whole human race in the range of their moral concern. But it is possible to go further, to include animals, then plants, and finally to experience 'a commonality with all that is'. This is the widest possible range of moral concern. To approach it requires a revolution in perception. We have tended to see humans – and male, rational humans especially – as autonomous rational beings who stand over against nature, for whose sake nature exists, who have dominion over nature, and use nature as a means to their own self-chosen purposes. It requires an inversion of thought to see humans as just one species among millions of others which have value, no more nor less than other species and individuals do, as parts of nature. Warwick Fox says,

---

[1] 'Self-Realisation: An Ecological Approach to Being in the World', p. 35, cited in *This Sacred Earth*, ed. Roger Gottlieb (Routledge, 1966, p. 436).

'We and all other entities are aspects of a single unfolding reality.'[2] And Bron Taylor quotes Christopher Manes thus: 'Evolution means that there is no basis for seeing humans as more advanced or valuable than any other species . . . evolution has no telos.'[3] What he means, I think, is that humans are not the goal of evolution; they are just one branch of an evolutionary tree.

For deep ecologists, 'the earth is primary and humans are derivative'. Humans are one part of a complex and interconnected ecological system 'in which all species ought to be able to fulfil their evolutionary destinies'.[4] They have a right to survive and flourish. For such a vision, the idea of human stewardship is flawed. Ruth Page says, 'Stewardship . . . is still too managerial a concept to support the kind of ecological ethic we need today.' And she says of the word 'dominion', 'I judge the word to be so dangerous that it is to be departed from in any contemporary doctrine of creation.'[5] Humans may have responsibility to help the parts of nature fulfil their potential as harmoniously as possible, but 'dominion' is too likely to lead to a lack of responsibility, feeling, respect, and care for the things of nature.

I think this call to an inversion of viewpoint, to a turning from anthropocentricity to a more cosmic moral vision, is enlightening and timely. But there are some questions to be raised. One main question concerns the sacredness of nature. Is the cosmos, or are the elements of the natural world, sacred? That is to say, are they worthy of reverence and worship?

Allan Brockway says, 'Human beings transgress their divine authority when they destroy or fundamentally alter the rocks, the trees, the air, the water, the soil, the animals – just as they do when

---

[2] In *This Sacred Earth*, ed. Roger Gottlieb (Routledge, 1966, p. 438).
[3] In *This Sacred Earth*, p. 547.   [4] Thomas Berry, in *This Sacred Earth*, p. 411.
[5] Ruth Page, *God and the Web of Creation* (SCM Press, 1996, p. 130).

they murder other human beings.'[6] But what if there is no divine authority – just the blind processes of chance and necessity? What is the basis here of any moral code with regard to nature?

The 'Nature red in tooth and claw' of the fifty-sixth stanza of Tennyson's poem 'In Memoriam' – bloody, indifferent, amoral, and blind – is rather different from Gaia, the Goddess Earth, who gives birth to her children, nourishes them, and binds them together in interconnected and beneficent harmony. The evolutionary process which exterminates millions of species and has, according to Bron Taylor, no purpose, seems quite different from an evolutionary process which, he implies, somehow gives to all beings the right to survive and flourish.

It is hard to see that a process as morally ambiguous as this can be intrinsically worthwhile. The Mother Goddess, where she is worshipped, after all is not wholly benign. In Indian traditions, Kali or Durga wears a necklace of human skulls and wades in blood. This image is not stressed by deep ecologists, who tend to write rather sentimentally, rather to James Lovelock's alarm, of Gaia as our Mother. It is, of course, quite possible to see the divine as ruthlessly destructive as well as creatively beneficent. One can worship out of fear as well as out of gratitude. But this does introduce a moral ambiguity into the idea of the divine which is alien to Christian reflection. It is not at all clear that, accepting such ambiguity, one is obliged, as deep ecologists sometimes seem to suggest, to grant to all beings in nature the right to survive and flourish.

There is, I think, good reason to distance a creator God from nature if we are to call God of supreme value, worthy of worship. Those who believe in God will think that there are many good

---

[6] Allan Brockway, cited in *This Sacred Earth*, p. 194.

things in nature and that its cruelties are either necessary or caused by evil finite choices. But though nature may in many ways reflect and express the beauty and wisdom of God, it is not itself supremely perfect by any test. It is at best an ambiguous sacrament of the divine presence. God alone is worthy of absolute worship — reverence for that which is without flaw or imperfection.

But can nature become perfect? The doctrine of the resurrection of the body entails that there is a resurrection of the physical environment of which bodies are parts. In the case of creatures who live and die, resurrection is often taken to mean a bringing back to conscious life. In the case of the physical environment, it will mean a bringing back to a form of existence free from its destructive tendencies. Can we begin to imagine that? We can imagine God knowing every element of physical reality. Such knowledge will presumably be held in the divine mind, without loss, forever. Wherever there are disvalues in nature, those will be sublated in God. That is to say, evil will be mitigated in its immediacy, transformed by the wider context of the divine knowledge within which it exists, and given meaning within the pattern of striving and overcoming of which it has been part.

We might think of such a reconciliation and harmony of all things as existing in the divine mind, which redeems time by sublating evil and transfiguring the temporal into the eternity of the divine life. The Christian vision of resurrection goes further. It promises a conscious sharing in this divine life to those who have lived in history. God will create 'a new heaven and a new earth', in which creatures can find that proper fulfilment which was so ambiguously expressed in this universe.

If such a thing is possible, it will be beyond the thermodynamic laws of the cosmos in which we now exist. Nature will not decay, no life forms will need to kill to live, and nature can become an unambiguous sacrament of the divine. Resurrection is the apotheosis of the cosmos, not just of human beings.

This does not decrease the importance of the present. It matters enormously what we now do in and to our world. If we can help new forms of beauty exist, they will exist in God and in the resurrection world that God creates. If we destroy beauty, then there are forms which could have been but now will never be – though God will surely enable many potentialities that were frustrated in this world to be realised in some form in the world to come. So hope for resurrection is ethically relevant to what we do now.

I have suggested that a Christian view has some natural affinities with the recent development of deep ecology. But there is sometimes hostility between those who declare allegiance to deep ecology and traditional Christians. This hostility has many roots. Some of them are brought out in one of the formative papers in the modern discussion of the theology of nature by the medieval historian Lynn White. In 1967 he wrote that 'Christianity bears a huge burden of guilt for the exploitation and destruction of the natural world',[7] which has now gone so far that some even speak of the 'end of nature'. He points out that in traditional Christian theology 'no item in the physical creation had any purpose save to serve man's purposes'. As Thomas Aquinas put it, 'The whole of material nature exists for man, inasmuch as he is a rational animal.' The section of his *Compendium of Theology* from which this comes is titled 'All creation is for man'.[8] White comments, 'Christianity is the most anthropocentric religion the world has seen.' If only human beings have immortal souls, and if God is concerned only for the redemption of humans, then the rest of nature has only instrumental value.

---

[7] Lynn White, 'The Historical Roots of Our Ecological Crisis', first published in *Science*, vol. 155, 1967.
[8] Aquinas, *The Light of Faith* (Sophia Press, 1993, sec. 148).

To make it worse, Genesis 1, 28 states that humans are to subdue and have dominion over the earth. The Hebrew term for 'subdue' is *kabash*, and the term for 'dominion' is *radah*. Those Hebrew words have the connotation of conquest, domination, even enslavement. And I fear the evidence is that this is how they have been interpreted for much of Christian history. Nature, including environment, plants, and animals, can be regarded as mere lumps of matter, to be used purely for human enjoyment. The denial of spirits in trees and rivers, which is characteristic of Christian faith, helped make it possible to treat nature as an object to be used rather than as an object of reverence and intrinsic value. Taken together, these factors have, White argues, led to the unfettered despoliation of the natural world and the alienation of human beings from their natural environment. Certainly, if one thinks that animals and natural objects have value which is to be respected, the historical record of Christianity is not good. So White argues that 'we shall continue to have a worsening ecologic crisis until we reject the Christian axiom that nature has no reason for existence save to serve man.'

White is himself a Christian, and his article is a confession of past inadequacies and a call to a renewed, more Franciscan, Christian vision of nature as a creation beloved of God. But it has been taken by many as an attack on Christianity, which is seen as the anthropocentric, dominating desacraliser of nature. Those who look for some spiritual vision which does not suffer from these disorders often look elsewhere, to some form of animism or Goddess worship or to what are characterised in a vague way as 'Eastern religions'. The earth can be seen as our Mother, Gaia, generating and sustaining life, or nature can be seen as a realm of spirits with rights or interests. Even process philosophy can take an animistic tone at times. All beings have 'a potential for richness of experience' which should be respected, John Cobb writes. It is not surprising that traditional

Christians feel some alarm at the apparent devaluation of person-hood, the attribution of quasi-personal characteristics and rights to natural processes which are normally thought to be non-sentient, and the identification of the divine with the morally ambiguous processes of evolution.

The frequent appeal by some writers to Eastern religions as super-ior sources of moral insight also does not generally commend itself to traditional Christians. Some writers have held that the 'Eastern' religions teach a greater unity with nature than the Abrahamic faiths, and than Christianity in particular. 'Asian faiths', writes Roderick Nash, 'never abandoned a sense of the unity of nature and subscribed to an ethical philosophy that did not begin and end with people.' This, it must be said, is a very selective presentation of Asian faiths. One of the most important Hindu religious systems is that of Sankhya, which views the world as consisting of *purusa*, spirit, and *prakriti*, matter. Matter may not be evil, but it deludes spirit into thinking that spirit is material. The way of release from suffering is to abandon all desires which attach one to the material, and to realise one's true nature as pure spirit. This is hardly a matter of seeing oneself as part of an organic whole.

In a similar way, in most Buddhist systems attachment to the material world inevitably brings suffering in its train, and one must renounce desire in order to attain *nirvana*, complete transcendence of nature. Moreover, in almost all Buddhist schools, being human is the only form of embodiment which gives the possibility of enlightenment, so that humans do have an immensely privileged position over other life forms (and men have greater privileges than women). It is just false that Asian faiths as such have a sense of the unity of nature which is non-anthropocentric.

There is, however, much to be learned from many Asian reli-gious traditions. We could well learn from Buddhism a sense of universal compassion for all sentient beings which has not been a marked feature of Christianity. We could learn a love of the rhythms and balance of nature from some aspects of Taoist thought. But just as Christian traditions are complex, so are Indian and Chinese traditions. It would be quite wrong to say either that Hindus and Buddhists see nature as something to be escaped from or that they see human lives as in organic unity with the natural world. The truth is that both these strands of thought exist in Asian traditions as they do in the Christian. If one is going to make a broad generalisation, it might be that the Indian traditions rarely conceive of nature as having a positive purpose, or as having some sort of lasting destiny (though some do). Insofar as Christians speak of resurrection, and of a new heaven and earth, they stress the materiality of the human person – and therefore the essential importance of its embeddedness in nature – more than most Indian traditions do. So those who find Eastern faiths intrinsically superior to the Christian in this respect simply have not examined the evidence adequately. Each tradition has much to repent of, and something to offer, in the search for a more adequate understanding of and ethical relation to nature.

It is because nature is 'red in tooth and claw' but also beautiful and awe-inspiring in its manifold striving for greater life that there is an important place for a distinctive Christian theology of nature. In that theology, nature itself will not be divine – nor will it be cruel or indifferent. It will be a process with an innate propensity towards developing beings of consciousness and responsible action who can share in the divine creative power to shape the world to endless forms of beauty and share in the divine comprehension of all created things.

In this process conscious responsible agents will have a special role. It will sometimes be the role of a conqueror, when it is the destructive power of earthquakes, tornadoes, animals of prey, and cancer viruses, which must be conquered. It will more often be the role of steward, guarding and creating beauty, and of enjoyer, delighting in that beauty. It will also be the role of worshipper, revering not nature in itself but God, the wise though often unfathomable intelligence which is known in and through nature and which expresses the divine nature in the refracted and multitudinous forms of the cosmos but which always remains beyond the ambiguities and imperfections of nature.

There is a proper anthropocentricity in Christian thinking about nature, but it is one of responsibility, not of dominance. Persons – and humans are the most fully developed persons on this planet – have the responsibility of creating, reverencing, and shaping nature. Because of their responsible freedom (not because of their species membership only), they have a moral dignity which seems unique to them. There is a proper sense of dominion. But, as Genesis 2, 15 suggests, humans are to tend or take care of the earth, not destroy or neglect it. Dominion is the delegated care of the world God creates with love, and for that stewardship all humans will be called to account. There is sacredness in nature, but it lies in its capacity to express in many finite forms transcendent divine perfection, and that capacity can be fully realised only when nature is liberated from its suffering and destructiveness, in a renewed creation (Romans 8, 19–23).

The Christian vision of nature is that although all things come to destruction, and although nature appears at times to be indifferent to the fate of the lives it generates, it can nevertheless be affirmed that the realisation of partly self-shaped communities of love is the final goal of creation. For nature can be in many of its aspects a sacrament of that perfect goodness which is God. In it we find a challenge to eliminate suffering and pain and shape it to forms of beauty and happiness, caring for all living things, so far as is possible, with compassion and delight. And within it there is the hope and promise of ultimate fulfilment, when the whole cosmos will be transfigured by God and filled with the glory of God as the waters cover the sea. Then nature will be, as it is not yet, the unambiguous sacrament of the divine, to be properly reverenced as a self-expression of the divine life and the final fulfilment of the divine purpose of creation. It is in such a hope for the realisation of nature as a true sacrament of God that a proper reverence for nature as God's creation can be securely grounded.

CHAPTER 13

Eternal Mind

The realisation that we have the power to destroy our planet, but that we also have an obligation to care for its good, points to something important about the created universe. Some people have thought that if there is a Creator, and since the Creator is good, everything in the universe must be for the best 'in the best of all possible worlds', as Voltaire put it in his novel *Candide*. But that is not what our world is like.

Our world is one in which new properties emerge from much simpler initial conditions. When our universe began with the Big Bang, about fourteen thousand million years ago, there was only an initial state in which there were no subatomic particles or complicated structures at all. From that state, as it expanded (or inflated) and cooled, many sorts of particles came into existence which physicists variously call particles or strings or fields of force. These were able to combine to form atoms, relatively stable structures, which in turn grouped into molecules, the basis of all the chemical elements that now exist. In the nuclear fusion at the heart of stars, heavier and more complex molecules were forged, and over aeons of time the amazingly complex structures of RNA and DNA, the basis of organic life, came into being. DNA is a code for building physical bodies in plants and birds and animals, and on this planet (and maybe on countless others) huge diversities of plant and animal life developed.

We now know that this development largely occurred through the mechanisms of mutation (changes in the make-up of DNA) and selection (the adaptation of organisms to their environment, which enables them to reproduce successfully). By the repeated application of those mechanisms, eventually some animals formed central nervous systems and brains. And finally, on the planet earth, the neocortex was formed in humans and for the first time enabled conscious intelligence and responsible freedom to exist.

This story of cosmic evolution is one in which over time more complex and more organised structures evolve by natural mechanisms and have ended up (so far, and on this planet) with intelligent, conscious life forms – human beings. It is possible that this has been a long sequence of accidents and purely chance occurrences. But that does seem hugely unlikely. It looks as if even at the beginning there was an inherent potentiality for consciousness, that the 'proper' way for the universe to develop was for it to realise gradually its true inherent potential.

Humans may belong to very early stages of the cosmic evolutionary story. But they are minds, with the capacity to understand, formulate, and realise values (worthwhile states). That gives them a special place, a special responsibility, to understand and direct their small bit of the cosmic process. They can understand where the universe is going and help it go that way.

Where is it going? As far as human imagination can foresee, it would be a worthwhile goal of the cosmic process to culminate in states that are of value just for their own sakes.[1] Until now, the evolutionary process has proceeded without its component parts consciously aiming at anything – just using mechanisms that work by churning out changes and selecting the most adequate

[1] A Christian exposition of such a goal-directed cosmic process has been provided by Teilhard de Chardin, in *The Phenomenon of Man* (Collins, 1959), now re-issued as *The Human Phenomenon*.

adaptations. It is remarkable that these mechanisms have led to the existence of minds which can take over conscious direction of the process. That does not seem to be an accident.

What we need to explain the process of cosmic evolution is something between pure accident and conscious design. We need a general purposiveness with an 'openness' in the system which allows genuinely creative responses to occur. In the early stages there is not much creativity but rather something more like inde-terminacy or what seems to be randomness. But as things get more complex, creative responsiveness becomes more marked, until with beings like humans there is fully conscious awareness and genu-inely free choices – still, of course, within limits set by the system.

In this cosmic process, there is a goal which is set even at the beginning of the process. One way of thinking of that goal is to see it as an envisaged future that exercises a general influence on the process. It is like a thought in the mind of the Creator which gives evolution a direction and goal. But since nature is open, and part of its purpose is to generate free, intelligent agents, there is a place for chance or randomness in nature and for finite free choices to emerge naturally from within nature – not as alien intrusions into a purely mechanistic and closed system of laws.

The Cosmic Mind generates nature, not as a perfect and wholly determined system, but as something more like a growing organic system, developing potentialities which were always inherent in it and leading to the emergence of communities of freely creative and responsively interacting centres of consciousness. We humans are free and interacting agents in a developing cosmos. The cosmic goal is set before us as a series of obligations or ideals, and we are free to 'improve' nature in accordance with these ideals, or to fail to do so. The fact that we are in danger of destroying our planet shows that we are failing. The fact that we feel (many us) that we are obliged to preserve the planet shows that we are aware of a purpose and goal central to our existence.

Not only must we appreciate and understand nature. We must counteract its destructive tendencies, which arise from its open, emergent, and initially unconscious character. We must enhance its positive tendencies, which are set by the goals enshrined in the divine mind. We must act for the frustration of evil and the enhancement of good. That is our primary purpose in this cosmos. It is in itself a spiritual practice. No allegedly religious or spiritual practice which ignores or denies this is worthy of the name.

Why did the creative mind choose this sort of emergent, open, developing universe, with all its seeming waste, frustration, destruction, and suffering? For some people, these features of the cosmos are enough to demolish any idea of God. But that is largely because they have a particular picture of God that is very unrealistic. They think that God is a person who knows everything, who can do absolutely anything, and who only wants to do good things. If you start with that picture, you have no chance of explaining why suffering and destruction exist at all. But why start with that picture?

So far, I have suggested that the idea of a supreme cosmic mind which originates the universe and intends to produce good things is both possible and plausible. This is one idea of what most people call God. But the idea of a mind might be misleading. It is misleading if it makes you think that God is a person who is a bit like human persons but just much more wise and powerful. What we are trying to think about is the ultimate origin of the whole universe. It is not really going to be much like human minds. Human minds get their experiences from their environment; they think of things one after another, and they are often at the mercy of all sorts of irrational feelings, impulses, and desires. God's experiences will not come from any environment, because no environment exists! God will not have irrational impulses or be subject to fits of depression or bad temper. The divine mind will be quite unlike any finite mind.

What I am really suggesting is that the source of the universe cannot be just blind, unconscious, valueless, and pointless matter. It cannot be matter at all, because it is that which brings matter into being. It must be beyond matter. It cannot be a finite mind either, because it is the source of all finite minds. It is reasonable, however, to think of it as possessing some form of consciousness, knowledge, value, and purpose. That is why I have called it mind, meaning that it is more mind-like than simply something quite unconscious and without value or purpose. But how can we think of a unique mind without any environment, without any developing character and knowledge, and without any relationship to other persons? As I shall go on to explain, the supreme mind may indeed create an environment to which it can relate and together with which it can in some sense develop. This will be the contingent creativity of the supreme mind. But it will also have an existence in itself, with a necessary and primordial nature beyond all relationship and development. This is the 'Actus Purus' of which Thomas Aquinas wrote – beyond human comprehension, unlimited, and beyond change, and yet the source of all change and finitude.

It must be a mind whose experience consists in thought. Thoughts in the primordial mind will be what give rise to this universe, and perhaps to many other universes too. But where do those thoughts come from? If mind is the origin and basis of everything, thoughts cannot come from anywhere but mind itself. Can we imagine a world of pure thoughts? I think we can, to some extent. Even we humans can think of many things that do not exist: unicorns, dragons, and centaurs, for instance. And we can imagine and even dream about things we have never done, like lying on a beautiful beach in the Bahamas. A supreme mind could think about every possible thing that could ever exist, whether those possibilities are necessary and primordial or creatively generated by mind itself. That is part of the meaning of the word 'omniscient'. A supreme mind would know every possibility, it would think of every possible thing that could ever be.

It would not have to think of one thing after another, as we do, however. It would not have to speculate or guess what things were like. Because possible states have no independent existence, they are rather like dreams or like drawings or pictures of real things that are not those things themselves. Being conscious of a real mountain is different from being conscious of a possible mountain. So possibilities are contents of the divine mind. They have real existence, and no doubt God appreciates and enjoys them for their intricate beauty and splendour. But there are no other actual consciousnesses in existence, so God does not share the divine thoughts with others or gain any new experiences from others.

There is no suffering in the mind of God who has not created any other beings, since God does not suffer, and the thoughts of the suffering of merely possible others are not real forms of suffering if those others do not really exist. So perhaps we can think of God as supremely happy in the contemplation of a huge array of mental contents, all of which are parts of the being of God. We have no idea of what this 'inner life of God' is like. It will be beautiful and amazing and intricate and glorious, but it is far beyond anything we can imagine.

We can say, however, that as it is the ultimate origin of all things, there is nothing else that can make it what it is. It cannot be brought into existence by anything else. In other words, by definition God can have no cause. And it obviously cannot bring itself into existence, because it would already have to exist in order to do that. Its primordial nature must be eternal. That means it must always have existed, not caused by anything. So its primordial nature just has to be what it is; and it could not have been different, because there was nothing to make it different. It will be an eternal mind.[2]

Many, probably most, classical philosophers have thought that there was such an eternal mind as the ultimate source and basis of physical reality. But what sort of mind could be eternal? We are at the edges of what we can imagine here, and the classical philosophers have disagreed among themselves. It is generally agreed, however, that this mind will know all possible things and will have the creative power to make thoughts actual; there must be such a power, because if something is possible, that means that it could exist. Some power must be able to make it exist, or it would not really be possible, and a reality which itself actually exists by necessity would possess in its own nature the power of existence. This is a power which could bring possibilities into actuality. An eternal mind could not, however, choose its own nature, or the primordial list of possible things that it knows. That is because it cannot create its own nature, and the primordial set of all possible things is part of its nature. This is a being of supreme knowledge and power. Some possible states will be of greater beauty, wisdom, or happiness than others, and a mind of supreme power will especially value and contemplate in itself all that is supremely good, all beauty, wisdom, creative power, and fullness of being. It is the cause of everything else that ever comes into existence, and everything else that exists depends wholly upon it at every moment. It is not an arbitrary tyrant or whimsical person. It is what the early philosopher Boethius called 'the unlimited ocean of Being', from which all other things flow. And it is not a blind, unthinking power.

---

[2] This is basically Aristotle's idea of the 'prime mover', the perfect mind, in *Metaphysics* lambda – except that Aristotle did not think that God created a universe and so was able to avoid the problem of how a changeless mind could create a contingent universe.

It is supreme consciousness and wisdom and is beyond all time, change, and decay. As the Bible says, it is what it is and will be what it will be (Exodus 3, 14), and before it and beyond it there is nothing.

There is, then, a widely accepted idea that the nature of ultimate reality is an eternal mind of supreme beauty, wisdom, and bliss. We are not at the mercy of a blind, indifferent alien force. We are created by supreme beauty and wisdom, and if we are to know reality as it truly is, we must see ourselves as creatures of ultimate mind and seek to know that mind in and through all its creations. This gives us an idea of what worship truly is. It is not some sort of cowering flattery of a being who likes to be told how great it is. It is the felt awareness of the upholding presence of mind in all things and the resolve to seek to know that mind more fully and help realise its purposes.

CHAPTER 14

Freedom and Necessity

It makes sense to think of eternal mind as contemplating a primordial set of possible states and enjoying beatitude in contemplating the most beautiful and glorious of those states. There is a sort of threefoldness in this mind. There is a primordial origin of all beings, an eternal expression of this in the conceived existence of possible states of being, and a contemplative activity of selecting the forms of the Good which exist among these possibilities and attending to them in one eternal act of loving appreciation. This gives one main meaning of the expression 'God is good': God is the eternal contemplation of the supreme forms of beauty and goodness. Christians may well think (St. Augustine did think) that it also gives one way of thinking of the idea of God as a Trinity, a threefold being who knows, wills, and loves the many forms of goodness and beauty that exist by necessity in the divine mind.[1] It is, of course, a very philosophical idea of the Trinity, but it enables us to see that the idea of God as Trinity is not some absurd mystery of irrational faith. It is a deep intellectual interpretation of the ultimate nature of reality.

This idea of God is produced by thinking of mind as the basis of all reality and imagining what such an eternal mind might be like. It is a thought experiment, and it is based on our own human experience

---

[1] This concept is developed more fully in my *Christ and the Cosmos* (Cambridge University Press, 2016).

of mind and an attempt to imagine what it might be like if something like a mind was the foundation of reality.

But this is not just an idle experiment. This God has to fit reality as we experience it. We can normally only experience the supreme mind as it is expressed in the universe. We are imagining that the universe is a making actual of a set of possible states which exist in the divine mind. It is not just the eternal expression of ideas in the mind of God itself, but also an external expression of ideas in an objective created order, which gives them a reality apart from the divine mind. Such an expression may be contingent and free, partly but not wholly determined by the necessary divine nature itself.

Since God is supremely good, it is natural to think that any states that are freely created by God will express some part of this goodness, its beauty and intelligibility, and awesome power. When we look at the natural world, this is what we see. But we also see that the created world is one of hardship, conflict, and often pain. Animals are incredible in their complexity and adaptedness, but many of them live by eating other animals and competing with one another for survival. Those are parts of the divine mind too, but such things surely cannot be freely chosen by a wise mind for their own sakes.

I think that the notion of 'free choice' is too simple to account for the expression of eternal mind in the physical universe. Mind chooses from a given set of primordial possibilities, which, I have argued, are not chosen but are necessarily what they are. The key abilities of mind – its ability to know, to choose, and to love – belong to it by necessity. Thus we can say that the goodness of eternal mind in its primordial nature is changeless and absolute. But it also has an expressive nature, a contingent expression in a world of time and space that is changing, developing, dependent, and contingent in many ways.

Because the expression of mind is partly necessary and partly creatively contingent, we can say that not everything that mind expresses is freely chosen, though everything has some reason for being as it is. As we think of the nature of our universe, with its mixture of beauty, wisdom, suffering, and hardship, and ask how such a universe could arise from God, we might suggest that when God creates, God does exercise free choice but also necessarily expresses many possibilities that are inherent in the divine mind. Though divine wisdom guides these possibilities towards embodying fragmented images of goodness, often they arise from necessary linkages between the divine ideas that are not wholly subject to any conscious choice. Divine intelligence is directed towards expressing images of divine goodness, but that process is constrained by divine necessity.

Maybe exercising creative power is what eternal mind does by nature – it is a creative power aiming at goodness but working through many sorts of possibilities, guiding them towards a goodness which is potential in them but needs effort to achieve. This would be a great exercise of creative power, to help shape things which are capable of it towards unique sorts of self-won goodness.

Would such a mind be good? It would be a creative power working for good. It would not make beings suffer because it enjoys seeing their suffering, so it would not be evil. It would aim at and ultimately achieve a state of unique beauty and goodness, achieved through creative striving. It would reinforce good tendencies and impede bad ones. I think it would be reasonable to say that such a being is good.

Our universe seems to involve a developing process in which increasingly self-organising entities are able to realise new values by effort and self-discipline. That means, however, that they may also fail to realise values because of inertia and inattention. The process, with its combination of beauty and suffering, looks like one of emergence through conflict and hardship towards a growing union with the supreme mind. Mind progressively realises the possibilities of its own nature by relating to a set of relatively autonomous entities which are embodied in a world of dangers and desires. It is the idea of God as a progressively self-unfolding mind which is characteristic of philosophical idealism and distinguishes this idea from the more Aristotelian idea that God remains wholly unmoved, unchanged, and in the end not personally related to the cosmos or to creatures within it. The Aristotelian idea of God, which has entered into much Christian tradition, is true of the primordial nature of God. But it neglects the way in which that primordial nature turns towards a created world in its expressive nature and relates to the world in suffering, compassion, and cooperating power.

The idealist picture is not of a wholly and unchangingly perfect God. Nor is it the more popular idea of a Person who consciously and freely chooses only good states when that Person could have chosen a much better world if he had wished to do so. There is too much chance, destruction, and suffering for that picture to carry conviction. The picture is of a self-unfolding mind which realises its own nature in relation to a world of many gradually developing self-organising entities. The aim of the process is to integrate these entities into the supreme mind. The supreme mind has the power to do that but cannot exercise its power coercively without destroying the creative freedom of the emergent order.

Many contingent forms of creativity and responsiveness are needed before a final integration and return of estranged beings to the Being of all – the unitive action of God – becomes possible. The question is not How can a loving God create so much suffering when it could have chosen otherwise? The question, rather, is Given that mind is the basis of the universe, what sort of mind could create a universe like this?

It seems that it would be a mind which necessarily generates, out of the possibilities of its own being, a dangerous and beautiful partly law-like and partly random emergent and open order from which self-directing subjects of experience emerge and have the capacity to realise conscious union with the supreme self.

In other words, the creation of a world like this was not a matter of absolutely free choice. This is how the divine mind expresses itself, in a combination of necessity and creative freedom. These are the possibilities it contains, and it is in the nature of a range of those possibilities to become actual. With the limited understanding we have, we cannot say what that range is or what freedom God may have within that range. Just as God cannot choose the divine nature, so God cannot choose in every respect how that nature is expressed. The cosmos in which we exist is a dialectical one in which the creation of the new and the destruction of the old seem to be intrinsically interconnected, in which there is a gradual development of autonomous life in a physical cosmos, and in which brute matter is progressively transformed into a sacrament of spirit. Given these conditions, we may think that at least in its existence and general nature, this cosmos must be as it is if we are to be the sorts of beings we are.[2]

What some theologians and philosophers have failed to see is that necessity need not be all-determining. If freedom is a real characteristic of finite beings, then there may be many possibilities which are not fully determined, and there may be many contingent factors within a scheme the general nature of which, though not all its particular features, is necessary.

---

[2] This idea of the progressive self-unfolding of Absolute Spirit converges with some modern scientific claims that the laws of nature must be what they are if intelligent life forms are to exist. While many scientists remain temperamentally averse to the idea that nature is purposive, I think that philosophical idealism actually supports a view of cosmic purpose with which scientific findings have a natural affinity.

Some philosophers argue that it would have been better for God to have determined everything so that everything was good rather than to allow a freedom which allows suffering to exist. But perhaps God had to allow freedom, for the expressive aspect of the divine nature compels God to relate to autonomous finite beings. That is not any sort of external compulsion. It is part of what the divine nature is, described in the Christian Scriptures as 'love', *agape*, or self-giving love (1 John, 4, 8), which implies relation to others. There are many things about God that have to be the way they are, but there are also some things about God that are contingent, that do not have to be the way they are. All that is needed to make sense of this is to postulate that God has two different sorts of properties; some are necessary and some are contingent.

An example would be that one person might love another and have no choice about that. Love is part of her nature. But she might express this love in many contingent and freely chosen ways: bringing roses home one day and cooking breakfast another day. We could say that she has to love but that love can be expressed in many different ways.

So we could say that God has to be conscious, wise, powerful, and good but can express the divine power in many different ways: by creating many different sorts of universes, for example. I think it makes perfectly good sense to say that God necessarily has to make some free choices about what sort of universe to create, because making free choices is a good thing. There is no logical problem about God being necessary in some ways but contingent and free in other ways.

Now we can say that perhaps God has to create some universe of freely creative and interacting minds if God is to express the divine nature as love. But if these created minds are really free, they can do things that God does not want them to do. God creates humans, for example, because God wants them to be free and happy. God does not want them to be destructive or to make one another unhappy. However, if God wants them to be free, God cannot stop them from being destructive, from doing things God does not want.

In a similar way, perhaps God has to create a universe in which matter develops emergent powers of its own, in order to become capable of expressing God perfectly. But this process of emergence must be self-organising and involve conflict and destruction as old structures are overcome and give way to new ones. As Hegel suggested, such a process may need to be dialectical: it is by the opposition of contrasting tendencies that a new synthesis is formed. For instance, the fusion of simple atomic structures in the heart of exploding stars is in one sense immensely destructive. But it gives rise to the generation of heavier atoms like carbon, without which organic life could not subsequently be formed. Out of the destruction of the old arises the creation of the new.

In a more social context, the principle of free speech may allow the genesis in a free society of hateful and spiteful statements. So a moral ideal gives rise to its opposite: an immoral outcome. Yet out of the interplay of these contrasting elements, a new synthesis may emerge for which freedom and wisdom can be balanced in a creatively new way. In a theological context, a God of love may generate created persons in order to express the divine love. But those persons will have their own relative autonomy and may express their creativity in opposition to the divine will for them. This will in turn, if the Christian perception of the Divine is correct, generate new forms of self-giving and redemptive divine love. So the processes of created being may be essentially dialectical, moving from thesis to its oppositional antithesis and offering the possibility of a greater synthesis – which in turn may form the thesis of a new dialectical triad. If we ask why the process is like this, we might simply have to say that it is the way in which the eternal mind progressively unfolds its own nature, as a truly creative, dynamic, and relational reality.

Where is God's freedom, then? It does not lie in God doing exactly what God wants, which would entail forcing things to obey the divine will. It lies in influencing the course of events so that some tendencies are reinforced and others are impeded. Just as finite persons influence one another, so God influences all finite things. They have real creative power, but God cooperates with, or counteracts, the way they exercise their powers, so that God's goals in creation are partly shaped by how creation itself acts but always remain oriented towards a final realisation of goodness.[3]

Is such a creation good? It has its source in a being of beauty and perfection, and it has its ultimate goal in union with that being. Not everything that happens in creation is good. But suppose that persons who emerge in a specific created universe would otherwise not have existed at all and that it is possible for them all eventually to share in an endless and unlimited good, the love of God. Then I think we could say that this universe is good; it is good that these persons exist. And they can help create forms of goodness – forms of excellence won by effort and discipline, cooperation, and compassion – that otherwise would not have existed.

My suggestion is that our world must exist with the general features it has, with its many conflicts and hardships, if we, with the specific natures and personalities we have, are to exist at all. Within

[3] A. N. Whitehead, for instance in *Process and Reality* (Macmillan, 1929), made the conception of divine influence, rather than divine determination of all things, central to his system of 'process philosophy'. For Christians, who believe that in Christ God submitted himself freely to the wills of evil men and women, such an idea of divine self-giving lies deep in the tradition. The system of process philosophy – with its apparent denial that God is the originating cause of all things, that there is a completion and fulfilment of the cosmic process, and that there exist substantial persons and things – is only one form of idealism, and it may be misleading to call my view a 'process' view. On the other hand, I would not cavil at that terminology, as long as the ultimate sovereignty of God, the ultimate triumph of goodness, and the ultimate reality of finite persons is affirmed.

this world, we each have a specific vocation, a specific purpose and destiny. We can forge new creative responses. We can have faith that the demands of Goodness are real and insistent. We can hope that final union with perfect Goodness is possible for us. And we can believe that love learned through our endeavours in a world that often seems far from the divine perfection will unfailingly lead to the fulfilment of our unique vocation.

PART III

Supreme Good

CHAPTER 15

Morality and Creativity

In Part II, I developed the idea of one supreme mind of the cosmos, a mind which is unique in existing and having its basic nature by necessity. For it is the necessary actual foundation for all possible worlds, and as such it can be conceived as a supreme form of consciousness. I argued that this mind unfolds and in a sense realises its own nature in creating and relating to other finite minds. The cosmos can be seen as an emergent, open, dialectical, developing, and relational organic unity which expresses the nature of ultimate mind as a supreme mind creating the possibility of new emergent and relational intrinsic values. Thus the cosmic mind has a dual nature: it is what it is by necessity, but it is also creatively free in relation to a contingent cosmos whose purpose is to realise communities of creatively intelligent and responsibly free persons.

In Part III, I will consider another aspect of the supreme mind: its nature as supreme value – 'that than which nothing greater [more valuable] can be conceived', as Anselm put it[1] – and the relation of this supreme value to the created cosmos. This will enable me to show how the rather abstract notion of a necessary ground of being broadens out into the idea of a personal reality with

---

[1] Anselm, *Proslogion* (1078), ch. 2. Anselm, like most medievals, thought that the highest value was changeless and passionless. After the European Enlightenment, many came to think that creative change and compassionate feelings were perfections, and idealist philosophers tend to agree with this. Naturally this will change the concept of God, but the new concept can still be based on an Anselmian definition of God.

which humans can have a conscious relationship – more like the Christian idea of God as the 'Father' of Jesus Christ. The discussion will draw out some of the moral implications of believing in such a God. It will also help me say more about the ultimate destiny of sentient beings within the cosmos. And it will enable me to show how this philosophical journey can provide a foundation for theistic faith in general and for a Christian form of theism in particular.

This part will be more explicitly Christian, and it will draw much of its material from Christian tradition. I do not want to claim that the philosophy of personal idealism can provide such specifically Christian insights on its own. Indeed I would accept that such a philosophy is capable of forming a foundation for a number of religious ways of thinking of the nature of ultimate mind. But this is a work of Christian theology as well as a philosophical treatise, and my aim is to show that the Christian faith, while not deriving from philosophical idealism, is a natural extension of many idealist insights, and that it contributes new and illuminating elements to a purely philosophical account. Those who are not Christian may wish to provide different accounts of how philosophical idealism may lead to a religious, or even to an expansive humanist, faith. I want to show how a Christian perspective can provide a rich experiential and affective context which gives existential force to what may otherwise seem to be rather abstract intellectual speculations.

If there is an ultimate intelligent mind which brings the universe into being, then this universe will have been selected for a reason. That reason ensures that there is a purpose to the existence of the universe. That purpose, in turn, gives a goal at which humans should aim. In this way ontology leads to morality. Then, as morality is conceived as the pursuit of a morally good purpose, questions arise as to the nature of this purpose and the conditions of its possibility in a universe like this one.

If philosophical idealism demands that we should learn to love the Good for its own sake, we need to know what the demands of Goodness are, what union with perfect Goodness will be, and how such union can be achieved. The enquiry into God is not a purely intellectual quest. It is also, and in a deeply integrated way, an enquiry into the nature of the good life for human beings in a universe such as ours.

If there is a Creator who creates for a purpose, one must begin by affirming that goodness should be a fulfilment, not a negation, of our truest being, our being as God intends it to be. The world is a place of danger and hardship. Our goal is to face these dangers, endure these hardships, and create positive goods out of the chaos of disordered desire. What is distinctive about us as human persons is that we are unique and partly self-directing agents of streams of thoughts, perceptions, feelings, and intentions. Moreover, we essentially exist in relation to other similar agents, from whom we learn, whom we imitate, and with whom we must cooperate to achieve our aims. Thus a basic moral aim is to realise the fulfilment of human beings who exist together in society and in a material environment.

If we are to fulfil our distinctive natures as human beings, we need to know what our distinctive natures are. If we believe that we are responsible agents who perceive, understand, feel, and will, and do so in close relationship to others, this means that we will fulfil our proper natures by seeking to perceive accurately, understand clearly, feel deeply and appropriately, aim at worthwhile and achievable goals, and help others do the same. It is not coincidental that these capacities – which are basically the capacities of knowing, feeling, and willing – reflect the primal nature of God, who understands all things, appreciates all that is good, and creatively wills our cosmos to exist.

In God these capacities are wholly and effortlessly realised. But in humans they are limited and difficult to achieve. In our perceptions we should appreciate the particularity and beauty of the world we apprehend, not taking such things for granted, seeking only our own pleasure. In our thinking we should seek to understand the world in which we live as fully as we can, avoiding prejudice and undue partiality of viewpoint. In our feelings we should be sensitive to the lives of other beings and not use them as means to our own gratification. In our intentions we should pursue creative and enriching goals, and cooperate with others to seek their well-being and not their harm. In these ways we will fulfil both our own personal lives and the personal lives of others.

Our distinctive human capacities, implanted in us by God, are our main clues to the sorts of lives we should seek to lead, and the sorts of ideals at which we should aim.[2] Those capacities should themselves be images, however partial and remote, of the character of God, for it is a basic Jewish and Christian doctrine that humans are made 'in the image of God' (Genesis 1, 27). The good life for humans, on such a view, will be lived in the imitation of God, so far as such a thing is possible. Reflection on the nature of God, especially as Christians take this nature to be revealed in the person of Jesus, will disclose the distinctive virtues which should mark human life and the distinctive ways in which those virtues should be expressed.

Christian accounts of the virtues often derive from Aquinas' *Summa Theologiae*.[3] That account is largely derived, in turn, from Aristotle's *Nicomachean Ethics*. In these works the virtues are human

---

[2] This insight is the foundation of the Christian moral tradition of 'Natural Law' – not the positive law enacted by political states, which may vary from nation to nation, but a universal law written into human nature, as intimating what our distinctive capacities and possibilities are. In the formulation I have given, this law will suggest ideals which fulfil human distinctive capacities, and it is for humans to work out what these capacities are and in what way they are best fulfilled.

[3] Thomas Aquinas, *Summa Theologiae*, questions 55–58.

dispositions which tend to produce happiness by the exercise of distinctive human capacities. Such dispositions include moral virtues like courage, temperance, friendship, and prudence, as well as the intellectual virtues like wisdom, understanding, and contemplation (*theoria*). In Aristotle, they often aim at a 'mean' state between excess and deficiency, so that one should be courageous without being either foolhardy or cowardly, for example. Aristotle assumes a generally teleological view in which humans have a 'proper' nature that expresses the natural excellence belonging to the human species as such. For him the highest virtue is that of 'contemplation', a purely intellectual capacity, for it is the most distinctive capacity of human lives (but maybe not of slaves, women, or barbarians).

For modern ethicists, this Aristotelian account is faced with two formidable difficulties. First, most modern non-theists reject the idea that there is a purpose for human life or an objectively proper way in which humans should live. We may indeed choose to be just and amiable. But we need not so choose, and if we do not, we are breaking no cosmic law. We are just choosing differently. We are not losing our 'true' humanity, because there is no such thing. Second, it is not clear that pursuing the 'middle way' will in fact lead to the highest happiness. Perhaps it does in general and in many cases. But a life of devotion to sensual pleasures can be happy and short, and who wants a longer life of boredom and self-denial? Aristotle admits that happiness is apt to be short-lived, confined to the affluent elite, and hard to attain, so many people may reasonably think that such a rare state is not worth the effort needed to attain it, since the effort may well fail in any case.

Aquinas is able to avoid these difficulties. He thinks that there is an objective purpose for human life, set by God. And he believes that there is a supreme happiness available to those who fulfil their purpose, in the afterlife if not in this one. So he can add to

Aristotle's list of moral and intellectual virtues the three 'theological virtues' of faith, hope, and love. One can have faith that the obligation to virtuous action is real and categorical and rooted in the purpose of God. One can have hope that a universal (not selfish or limited) fulfilment is possible, since God promises it. And one can seek and to some extent experience the passionate love of God which makes real a conscious and personally transformative relationship to the author and sustainer of all creation.

In my view, Aquinas gives the more coherent account of the seriousness and pressing nature of the most natural moral beliefs of human beings. While accepting his account in general, and accepting that there are many diverse virtues that need to be carefully examined, I will explore, in a slightly different way, five especially important virtues which seem to follow directly from consideration of the nature of God, as it is understood in philosophical idealism, an idealism extended and qualified by insights drawn from the Christian faith. The divine properties I have in mind are the properties of creativity, sensitivity (appreciation), and understanding, which belong to God as the creator of all, who appreciates (or loves) and understands (or contemplates) both the divine being and the created order. I will also consider the properties of synergy (cooperation) and empathy (compassion), which belong to God as one who actively relates to and passionately feels the actions and experiences of finite persons. I shall consider them in order and begin with the virtue of creativity.

This virtue seems to follow from the fact that God is known to us as creator, as the one who brings the cosmos into being in order to fulfil a purpose which is good. It also follows from the fact that purpose and creativity, displayed in the exercise of responsible freedom, are distinctive qualities of human personhood.

Strange as it may seem, creativity as a primary value has not been as greatly stressed as it might have been in Christian tradition. It is probably the twentieth-century philosopher A. N. Whitehead (especially but not only in *Process and Reality*) more than any other philosopher who has stressed the primary value and importance of creativity, in the sense of bringing into being something radically new. For Whitehead, each 'actual occasion' or event that exists gathers together data from its immediate past and projects into the future something that is a product of its own creative power. Whether or not one accepts this idea of reality as consisting of momentary 'actual occasions', the idea that something creatively new can come to be – that this is a perfection, not a defect, and that finite persons can have, to a limited extent, such creative power – is a valuable idealist contribution to thinking about God. And one can accept it as such without being committed to all the theses of process philosophy.

There have been periods of history when creativity was not especially valued. Indeed, it has often been thought that conformity to tradition or repetition of some primal pattern of life is the greatest human virtue. There is a certain amount of truth in such attitudes, for God can be thought of as the supreme primordial goodness, the Good itself. In that sense, all human striving can do is produce a series of imperfect copies of some aspect of the eternal and unchanging Good.

Traditional ideas of God, derived from aspects of the thought of Plato and Aristotle, have seen God as changeless and impassible, as not needing to create any universe in order to bring into being anything new, and as not being affected by anything that happens in a created universe. On these views, creation cannot add anything to the being of God. Creation is purely for the sake of creatures who change but whose changes leave God exactly as God always was and always will be, whether or not those creatures exist. Perfection is a sort of changeless contemplation of the Good. As Aristotle put it, God is 'self-thinking thought',[4] a being whose perfection rests simply in contemplation of its own changeless perfect nature.

Idealist thinkers generally challenge this idea of perfection and therefore also challenge this idea of a God who is supremely perfect. Why should perfection be thought of as an unchanging and unchangeable state? Such a view would entail that bringing something new into being by creative effort is not part of perfection, or is not of great value for its own sake. But if you think of a composer or an artist who brings into being music or paintings that have never before existed, which reveal patterns of sound and colour which are totally original with them and develop previous patterns in new ways, it might begin to seem that such creative activity is, after all, of great value. Originality is something one may prize, and the effort and talent that is thereby realised is one of the most satisfying excellences in human life.

The evolutionary perspective is one that stresses that new things can develop, that the complex can grow from the simple (even though theists believe that this requires direction by a supreme intelligence), and that not everything is predetermined by a prior reality so that there is truly nothing new under the sun.

The evolutionary perspective is also closely related to a sense of historical particularity, which developed in Europe with the rise of critical history and of empirical science. For Anselm, as for Plato, the eternal ideas in the mind of God were more real than their merely temporal copies, and the ideal goal of human life was to move from the temporal and changing to the eternal and timeless. In Christian philosophy, particular individuals were thus in a sense less real than their eternal archetypes (or 'essential natures'), so that 'humanity' was more real than 'particular human beings'.

---

[4] Aristotle, 'Noesis noeseos' – a 'thinking of thinking' or a thought that thinks itself; we might say a perfectly beautiful being which has the highest happiness in contemplating its own beauty.

The sense of historical particularity reverses that perspective and states that individual events that happen in time are more real than eternal concepts, which are relatively abstract and unreal. We may prefer to say that each is real in different ways. But the emphasis on the historical and particular as having its own distinctive reality and being worthy of contemplation in and for itself was a radical conceptual revolution. It means that time and individuality have an intrinsic importance of their own and are not just ultimately dispensable means, or even distractions, on the path to the contemplation of the eternal.

Such a change of perspective from privileging the universal to accepting the full reality of the particular can lead, and does seem to have led, to a complete denial of the eternal and essential, and eventually to a form of materialism which denies that there is any non-temporal or purely conceptual reality. But this does not have to be the case. For it is precisely the life of the mind, not the processes of the material, that has a sense of the temporal, that is uniquely individual, and that is in a continual flowing process. Creativity essentially involves change – the evolution of the new which builds on but transcends the already existing – and it involves particularity, because what I create is uniquely my product, to which I contribute my unique talent and expression.

So with the primordial mind of God, if God creates a universe, which begins and perhaps ends in time, then God creates something new, something additional to the being of God itself. Some new content of the divine mind is actualised.[5] God must change creatively, and if God is truly a creator, then God becomes what God need not have been. Knowledge of the contingent must itself be

---

[5] This may seem a controversial point to those used to thinking that God is essentially immutable. I have defended it more fully in *Christ and the Cosmos* and elsewhere. But the crucial question is this: is creative change necessarily an imperfection? If not, then the doctrine of divine immutability can at least be qualified to allow some notion of real contingent divine activity too.

contingent. Thus the existence of a contingent universe changes God. As the German philosopher and Lutheran pastor Johann Gottfried Herder put it, the universe progressively unfolds what has always been potential in it. Creativity becomes a great value when the universe is perceived to be an evolving and emergent process within which the emergent striving of human beings can be seen as a basic virtue, an essential human excellence.

It must not be forgotten, of course, that becoming is the expression of being. That is, the process of creative change is not chaotic or haphazard and completely unforeseeable. There are parameters of change and emergence. There are primordial depths of eternity and necessity in Being, though they are largely hidden from human thought. To put it in the language of religion, ultimately God must be, changelessly must be, what God is – wise, compassionate, and blissful in being. But this eternal reality is not some extra layer of being, separated from the creative flow of the temporal. It is rather the form of the temporal, the changeless nature, that is expressed in continual change – just as changeless wisdom may be expressed in manifold and diverse wise decisions in ever-new contexts. So, we might say, in a rather paradoxical but certainly not contradictory way, that God is changelessly and essentially creatively free. In seeking to be creative, humans may cooperate with the creativity of God. In doing so, they both add new elements to the divine knowledge and enable the divine activity to be expressed in novel ways. It is in this way that idealism evokes a particular view of the human-divine relationship that gives rise to a distinctive view of what the moral life of humans really is.

CHAPTER 16

Philokalia

Creativity is an important moral ideal for how human life is to be lived. The moral life is not, however, one of ceaseless activity. There is an important place for contemplation too. This need not be a religious sort of contemplation of God. It can properly be the appreciation and understanding of the ordinary and particular values of everyday life and of the natural world. I have considered first the virtue of creativity. The second and third human virtues that I shall consider are those of sensitivity (or appreciation) and understanding. God is known to us as one who has perfect wisdom, who understands all that is, including the hearts of men and women. And God delights in the beauty and order of the created cosmos. The Book of Proverbs speaks of the eternal wisdom of God, personified as Lady Wisdom: 'rejoicing in his [God's] inhabited world and delighting in the human race' (Proverbs 8, 31). So created persons should seek to understand and delight in the cosmos that God has generated.

Part of the good life for humans is learning truly and intensely to appreciate and understand more fully the values of truth, beauty, and goodness as they are found in the natural world which they inhabit. The simple contemplation of a beautiful landscape is something that can fill the mind with a distinctive pleasure that is calm and serene. On hearing a Mozart symphony, one can learn to understand how the harmonies are formed, the instruments combined, and the musical themes developed, and so appreciate the music in a more intellectually saturated way. On coming to understand the theory of relativity, one can discover the beauty of numbers and imaginatively explore the structures of space and time, finding excitement in the way one can appreciate the intricate complexity of the natural world.

It is not the case that one of these ways of appreciation and understanding is 'better' than the others. There are different degrees of intellectual understanding interwoven in various ways with different forms of sensuous appreciation. Feeling and thought are both engaged in all acts of appreciation. Both can be cultivated, by taking the time to attend to the natures of things as they present themselves to us and finding in them a non-possessive, non-egoistic loss of self by entering into their objective goodness.

Though there is no hard and clear distinction between appreciation and understanding, appreciation is more concerned with the affective tone of experience. It is concerned with the feelings of attraction or aversion that are aroused when we apprehend something. Such feelings are not purely subjective, as though they had nothing to do with the nature of the objects themselves. They are, or should be, feeling responses that are appropriate to the nature of things, and thus they give a sort of knowledge of things that is in itself not conceptual. It is more like acquaintance with or even love for another person, which gives a knowledge of that person not open to others but is real and objective nevertheless.

One could speak of 'affective knowing', a distinctive form of knowing by participation in the being of another. It requires an openness to their being, a sensitivity to the natures of things. So there is a sort of discipline of the feelings, as one shapes oneself into the sort of person who can be open and sensitive and not diverted by the undue influence of personal desires and proclivities.[1]

Understanding is more concerned with thought, with forming concepts for describing and relating things and interpreting their natures. The formation of concepts is fraught with difficulty. Our concepts are almost always in some natural language, and that language has a history of constant change in which words can change their meanings quite radically over time. Words can also be interpreted very differently in different linguistic subgroups. So it is not helpful to speak of the 'one correct meaning' of a word, even though dictionaries exist to record some widely accepted meanings and to try to present a certain standard usage in cases of dispute.

So without some sophisticated mathematical concepts there are things we simply cannot understand, in quantum physics for example. And it is probably true that many philosophical disputes arise because we just have not thought of precise, accurate, and clarifying concepts which might enable us to cut through the disputes (I am thinking of long-standing arguments about 'free will', 'mind and matter' and 'God', for example). Understanding is a continuing search for better ways of thinking about the things we experience which give us a more comprehensive, coherent, and fruitful grasp of how things really are. And I suspect that we will probably never achieve a completely comprehensive, coherent, and fruitful view.

We might say that concepts do not mean things. People mean things by using concepts, but what they mean can only be discovered by seeing how they use and relate vast webs of concepts which together comprise a general set of values and ways of seeing the

[1] This need for a disciplining of the feelings is stressed by John Cottingham, especially in *Why Believe?* (Continuum, 2009).

world of their experience. Sometimes we might need to share in that web of concepts to understand more fully what they mean.[2]

This is not meant to be a defeatist remark, as though all understandings are relative (without objective truth) or that there is no difference between poor and good understandings of a given topic. It is meant as a reminder that understanding is a difficult and many-levelled process. To possess a good understanding of something is a virtue, a distinctively human excellence. Like appreciation, it requires a certain humility, sensitivity, and self-knowledge. In philosophy, as Socrates said (according to Plato), the person of greatest understanding is one who realises that they fully understand very little. Nevertheless, greater understanding is a moral goal that is always worth striving for. It is an asymptotic ideal, the full possession of which probably belongs only to God.

The ideals of appreciation and understanding can be seen by idealists as imitations of that perfect appreciation and understanding that exists in the divine mind, and so as participations in the divine wisdom. Possibly, then, the divine may illuminate human minds through the inspiration of human feeling and thought – though it is as well to be very cautious about human claims to have been so inspired. Yet it would be reasonable to take as an ultimate goal of the moral life a fuller participation in divine wisdom, bliss, and intelligence, and so to think that this is an attainable goal after all. This is a distinctive view of the moral life and its goal that the philosophy of personal idealism underpins.

The three virtues of creativity, appreciation, and understanding are moral ideals which arise from consideration of the nature of the

---

[2] This is a point made in some later writings of Wittgenstein, which have been collected and edited by G.E.M. Anscombe in *Philosophical Investigations* (Blackwell, 1974). Wittgenstein emphasised that language is a social activity that is a constitutive part of a form of life and not a neutral catalogue of purely objective facts. It is living and dynamic, making many diverse forms of understanding possible.

supreme mind and its purpose for the created cosmos. They are suggested by the nature of that mind as one who creates for the sake of realising new forms of value and for the sake of appreciating and understanding them. They are, I think, virtues which help define what the good life is for a human person. These virtues cannot be cultivated in solitude, for persons do not exist in isolation. Few forms of creativity, modes of appreciation, or kinds of understanding would be possible without participation in a social complex with its own history and set of basic values. Each person needs to work cooperatively (synergistically) with others and to have a deep feeling for and understanding of other persons.

Thus two other virtues, the social virtues of cooperation and compassion, can be seen as essential to the existence of any society of minds. The virtues must be ideals for all persons, not just for one or a few privileged individuals, and justice consists in aiming at the highest realisation of such ideals for all, without exception, in a community of mutually supportive persons. The supreme mind taken on its own would not possess, even in perfect form, the virtues of cooperation, compassion, and justice, simply because there is no community present and no need in the divine life for cooperation or compassion. Nevertheless, it may be thought to be a divine perfection in God to create societies of finite persons in relation to whom divine cooperation and compassion can be effectively realised. Such cooperation and compassion would still need to respect the proper autonomy of finite personhood and of the physical cosmos from which such personhood emerges, and this suggests an 'influencing' rather than a 'determining' view of divine activity in relation to finite persons. Such creative activity would make possible a communion of personal beings which, idealists might think, would be a fulfilment of the divine nature, even if is not an obligation or necessity for God to create such a communion. The question of whether such a form of fulfilment for God may be a necessity is hard, probably impossible, for humans to decide. But there can be little question that in the cosmos as it actually exists, the supreme mind will exercise cooperation and compassion. For it is part of the moral perfection of created persons to establish and sustain societies in which friendship can flourish, and friendship with God should complete, not undermine, such social relationships.

Most idealists believe that human minds cannot be regarded as isolated and wholly autonomous. The twelfth-century Indian idealist Ramanuja said that finite selves and the material universe together constitute 'the body of the Supreme Lord'.[3] This image implies that the experiences of finite selves become parts of the all-inclusive experience of the supreme mind, and thus organs of experience for the supreme spiritual reality. The actions of finite selves become expressions of the all-encompassing creativity of the supreme mind, and thus realisations of potentialities inherent in the supreme spiritual reality.

The image of selves as the body of the Lord, which is remarkably similar to the Christian image of believers as parts of 'the body of Christ',[4] stands in need of qualification from a Christian viewpoint. Many finite experiences, like the pleasure felt by a torturer, cannot be attributed to God. Yet being known by God, they enter into the experience of God. As such, they must carry an element of 'judgment' or censure, and thus a distancing from the perfection of the divine mind. The realisation of certain possibilities in the divine mind is due to consciousnesses other than and often alienated from the divine mind itself.

---

[3] Ramanuja, 'Brahman has individual souls for its body' (*The Vedanta Sutras*, trans. George Thibaut, in *Sacred Books of the East*, Motilal Banarsidass, 1962, vol. 48, p. 132).
[4] Romans 12, 5: 'We, who are many, are one body in Christ.'

Christian idealism is therefore distinguishable from absolute or non-dualistic forms of idealism in that, as in the idealism of Ramanuja, an irreducible alterity and relationship exists between the supreme mind and finite persons. There is a diversity-in-unity such that the ideal towards which the cosmos is meant to move is a mutual indwelling of many diverse experiences and actions. This is a complete cooperation of actions and sharing of experiences, by which the primordial mind is expressed in and through the diverse minds of finite beings. Those beings in turn contribute to the divine experience by their own freely creative choices. For Christians, however, this is an ideal to be fully realised only at the end of this world's time. In this universe, there is a possibility, which has unfortunately become actual, that the ideal communion of being will be broken and that finite minds will choose radical autonomy and individualistic self-will rather than extended sympathy and cooperation.

In such a world 'the will which is above us and higher than ours'[5] will not be adequately realised solely in and through the self-realisation of many finite wills. Union with such a will becomes an ideal which is hard, and maybe impossible, to realise and which comes to seem like a demand of the moral life. It will not, however, be an arbitrary command of some superior power. It will be an intimation of what a perfected life can be, bringing with it a hope that our failures will not render such a life completely beyond reach. This is one form of the Christian Gospel, that God will bring to perfection what we cannot achieve but which remains the proper form of our self-realisation as members of the body of the Supreme Lord.

John Stuart Mill longed for the growth of universal sympathy and creative human cooperation, of what he called 'the feeling of

---

[5] F. H. Bradley, *Ethical Studies* (Clarendon Press, 1927, p. 159).

unity with all sentient beings', which he said should be 'taught as a religion'.[6] But we may well doubt that such a thing is humanly possible. Immanuel Kant wrote that 'We can never hope that man's good will will lead mankind to decide to work with unanimity towards this goal.'[7] And David Hume says, 'There is no such passion in human minds as the love of mankind.'[8] The hope for universal sympathy is probably impossible for human beings as they actually are. Christian idealism brings to that hope the belief that universal Spirit will make the realisation of a truly universal sympathy actual even for human beings who are presently filled with hatred and the spirit of divisiveness, though maybe not in the world as it is presently constituted. It would need some sort of moral reconstitution or renewal. If such a thing were possible, then we could see humans not as the weak and corrupted wills they so often seem to display, but rather as always possessing the inmost possibility of becoming unique contributors to the self-expression of the mind of God, and therefore as proper objects of respect, compassion, and hope. It is in this sense that moral commitment and moral hope can be given a firm metaphysical foundation in a philosophy which makes a continuing personal life beyond this world a real possibility.

[6] John Stuart Mill, *Utilitarianism*, first published 1861, ch. 3.
[7] Immanuel Kant, *Religion within the Limits of Reason Alone*, 1794, book 3.
[8] David Hume, *An Enquiry concerning the Principles of Morals*, 1751, sec. 2, part 1.

CHAPTER 17

The World to Come

In Part I, I argued that the core of human personhood is a non-material unitary subject of experiences and agent of creative and morally free actions which has traditionally been called the soul, although this word is understood in a misleading way by many. In Part II, I argued that there is a supreme non-embodied mind which, like the human soul, has knowledge and acts creatively, even though it is dimensionally greater than any human soul. In this part, I have considered the basis of morally good actions as the realisation of distinctive values – set by the supreme mind as ideals for human souls to pursue – that would not otherwise exist. And I have suggested that the full realisation of such values might not be possible without the continued existence of personal lives beyond this world. Many religions have supposed that human souls can exist beyond the death of their physical bodies, and this seems, if the arguments already given are accepted, to be possible. There already is at least one non-embodied mind, and it seems that a non-material soul does not necessarily need to be embodied.

Nevertheless, most Christian theologians believe in the resurrection of the body, and not in the immortality of the soul. There is good reason for this, since the idea of an immaterial soul which is the true inner self, and the destiny of which is to be liberated from the body and live in a purely spiritual realm, is not one which is characteristic of Jewish, Christian, or Muslim mainstream thought.

Plato called the body the tomb of the soul, and many religious traditions make it their ultimate goal to escape the limitations and ills of the physical body. That was not a Jewish ideal. In early Hebrew thought, the soul (*nephesh*) was breathed into the body as a principle of life. It was characteristic of all living, breathing animals, not just of humans. When the body stopped breathing, that was the end of life. For many Jews there was no life beyond death, and it is still possible to be an orthodox Jew and deny any form of afterlife.

Nevertheless, a belief in life in the world to come entered into Jewish thought, and when it did, it was usually in terms of some sort of embodied existence. Jesus agreed with the Pharisees that there was a place of the dead, *Sheol*, and that figures like Moses and Isaiah continued to live in a more attractive realm, Paradise (Jesus was said to have talked with them on a hilltop).

Jesus also thought that there would be a resurrection of the body. But though he of course is believed to have experienced resurrection, there was no agreement among Christians on what sort of embodied existence this was. There have probably always been those who thought that the afterlife body would be the same as the earthly body, but made free from disease and decay. Perhaps the resurrection would take place on this earth, but only when earth had been transformed by God after 'the great and terrible Day of the Lord'. The dead would rise in healthy, shining, and glorious bodies and carry on with their lives in an earth much as before, except that their world would now be filled with the clear and vivid presence of God and of the saints and angels.

Paul, however, is not so sure. In the classic Pauline passage, 1 Corinthians 15, he writes, 'Flesh and blood cannot inherit the kingdom of God' (verse 50). That pretty clearly implies that whatever the resurrection body is, it will not be flesh and blood. That means it will not be physical. It will not be the same body that people have during earthly life. He says of the body, 'It is sown a physical body, it is raised a spiritual body' (44). The words in Greek are *soma psychikon* and *soma pneumatikon*. These words are hard to translate, for they literally mean 'a psychic, or mind-like, body' and a 'spirit-like body'. I have suggested that possibly the 'psychic' refers to the mind as it engages with the world of the senses and that the 'spirit' refers to the mind as it engages with more abstract conceptual ideas or with the spiritual reality of God. In any case, Paul makes a distinction between the body that is involved in earthly sense experiences and another sort of body that is not so involved.

Paul writes, 'You do not sow the body that is to be, but a bare seed . . . but God gives it a body as he has chosen, and to each kind of seed its own body' (37 and 38). The physical body is like a seed which is to germinate in the world to come. In that world, God will bring the seed to maturity, giving it a new kind of body, appropriate to each seed.

If we ask what kind of body this will be if it is not a physical body, Paul just says, 'Fool!' which appears to put an end to the debate. But that it will be radically different does not seem to be in question. He does, however, also say some positive things about the spirit body. It is imperishable, immortal, glorious (beautiful), and powerful. Such characteristics cannot belong in this physical universe. A basic law of our universe is the second law of thermodynamics, the law of entropy. It states, to put it briefly, that everything decays and that the whole physical universe will one day run down and cease to exit. Perishability is a basic law of our universe. So if spirit bodies are to be imperishable, they cannot exist in the physical universe at all.

For Paul, it seems that there is a spiritual universe, whose laws are quite different from the laws of this physical universe and in which we, the very same persons, will exist and come to possess to the full all the capacities we had on earth, but in a more vital and developed form. Then we will see our earthly lives as mere seeds which can only fully produce what is potential in them when they come to exist in a spirit universe.

The resurrection of the body, according to Paul, is not the resuscitation of these physical bodies at some future time. It is the entry of human persons into a quite different spirit universe, finding themselves in non-physical bodies with vastly expanded capacities and possibilities of existence. This is certainly an attractive idea. Of course, we should not forget that it is not just an idea. It is based on Paul's reflections on the resurrection of Jesus, who, he believed, appeared as a blinding light, not a physical body, on the Damascus road.[1] Jesus did appear as a physical body to the disciples, but even then, according to the Gospels, he appeared for short periods behind locked doors, was not recognised immediately, and disappeared again instantaneously. This was no ordinary physical body. On available testimony, it seems to have been a fully physical appearance of a reality that was already beyond the laws of the physical universe. We might say that the miracle of Jesus' resurrection was not that his physical body came to life again and walked out of the tomb. It was that his physical body disappeared and that after that there were, for a relatively short time, a number of appearances of his spirit body (his 'risen body') in various physical forms.

If we take these accounts seriously, we shall have to say that there are spirit bodies in a spirit universe and that humans will be given such bodies as fulfilments of the potentialities present in their

[1] Acts 9, 3.

physical bodies on earth. This, however, raises the difficult philosophical question of whether it is possible for the very same person to have, successively, very different kinds of body in very different universes. It is, surprising as it may seem, more like reincarnation than like reduplication. Some physicists have fantasised that in the far future intelligent beings will have the capacity of re-creating the DNA of all presently existing humans.[2] Then they can bring these humans back to life – like the dinosaurs brought to life in 'Jurassic Park' – and that will be the resurrection of the dead. But such a scenario would completely miss the point of the New Testament view of resurrection. The New Testament does not want us to have our old bodies back again; it wants us to have different bodies, spirit bodies, in a spirit-filled universe.

But is such a thing even logically possible? If we are to be the same persons but with different bodies, our identity cannot consist in our physical make-up. It must lie in something distinct from the physical. Of course my body is important to me. It helps shape my character and sets limits on my capacities. My brain, in particular, must be in good working order if I am to have anything like a normal human life. If I am ill, I cannot function as well as I should. If my brain becomes disordered, my conscious life will be seriously affected. There is no question that my physical body and brain are necessary to my living a properly human life on earth. Body and mind go naturally and properly together, and do not function in different parallel universes.

We can, however, properly pose the question Could the mental and physical components exist apart? The body obviously can exist without the mind and without consciousness. It often does. But can consciousness and mind exist without a body or, more relevantly,

---

[2] See Frank J. Tipler, *The Physics of Immortality* (Doubleday, 1994).

without a brain? It is harder to find instances when it does so, but I think it is easy to think of it doing so. I can, as a thought experiment, imagine my brain and body disappearing while I go on thinking and even perceiving things around me. There are difficulties about this: how would I have visual perceptions without eyes or brain? But they might just spontaneously appear. After all, we can induce perceptions by stimulating the brain electrically, so eyes are not necessary. What about the brain? With the present causal laws of the universe, the brain is necessary to perception. But those laws are contingent; they do not have to exist. If the laws were different, we could still have perceptions. We could be, for instance, disembodied consciousnesses which received perceptual data by some form of telepathic communication from a more advanced mind. We do not think this happens. But it could happen. It is a logical possibility. And the point is that consciousness may depend on many things, but it does not have to depend on the precise physical laws that governed the formation of our brains. In other words, the mental does not necessarily depend on the physical – though I have no doubt that our minds do, as a matter of contingent fact, depend on the working of our physical brains.

We might think of it like this: God is, or possesses, a non-embodied mind. God is a consciousness which is fully aware of everything that ever happens – God is all-knowing. If so, then God has mental properties without having any physical properties. This is easily imaginable, and I think it is a fact. So it seems possible that humans too could have mental properties without having any physical properties. During life, this does not happen. But when our brains die, we may go on having mental experiences. Whether we do or not is a matter for investigation. No philosopher or neuroscientist can deny that possibility just by definition.

When humans die, they may continue to have memories and a sense of their own identity. But if they are to have new experiences, to communicate with other persons, and to be identifiable by other persons, they will have to have something like bodies. Bodies are the means by which information about an environment is selected and presented to consciousness, bodies are the means by which others can identify us as continuing individuals, and bodies are the means by which we can act and do things in an environment. Bodies are important to beings like us, precisely because we are continuing social individuals who learn from and act in an external environment.

But is it important that we should always continue to have the same body? Most of us do not continue to have the same body throughout our earthly lives anyway. We start off with the body of a baby, and we end, if we are lucky, with the body of an old person. These are not the same, and every atom of our body changes during the course of our lives. There is, of course, a continuity in time and space. We do not disappear in one place and suddenly reappear in another. But we could do so, and we would soon get used to the experience, though it would seem odd at first.

Suppose that I instantaneously change from a child to an old person, or suppose I have a terrible accident or illness that changes my appearance completely. My body would have changed perhaps out of all recognition. But I could still be the same person. I would have very much the same memories, thought patterns, feelings, and hopes. I would know that certain experiences happened to me that no one else knows anything about but that I am the same person now as the one who had those experiences.

There is, then, reason to think that we could live in a different form of body, as long as we retained the same mental content and sense of continuing identity. Like Paul, I think we cannot now know what form of body that will be, except that it will have some causal continuity with any earthly body that we had and that it will find itself able to explore possibilities that were present in the earthly body but were inhibited or limited in certain ways. And it will perhaps find itself, at least in the first instance, in a community of other persons with whom one had relations on earth.

When will such a resurrection occur? The New Testament contains different views about this, but there are some hints about beliefs that were held at least by some in the early Church. Jesus spoke to Moses and Elijah on a mountain (Mark 9, 4). He said to the penitent thief, 'Today you will be with me in Paradise' (Luke 23, 43). The creedal belief that Jesus descended into Hell (actually, *Sheol* or *Hades*) is based on a text that speaks of Jesus preaching to 'the spirits in prison' – that is, the dead (1 Peter 3, 19 and 4, 6). At least some of the dead speak, hear, and live in the presence of Christ, while others exist 'in prison' or a place of punishment.

These passages fit a belief that some form of resurrection, or existence in a spirit body, occurs immediately at death. There are various sorts of post-death existence, from a punishing and purifying fire to the bliss of Paradise. Doctrines of Purgatory and eternal Hell were later developments of this belief, but we may think, and I do think, that it is more consistent with the idea of a God of unlimited love to think that punishments can always be ended by repentance, even in the afterlife.

So we may think, like the early theologian Gregory of Nyssa, that there are various sorts of existence, and various sorts of bodies, in the spirit world. It is God's will that all should be saved (1 Timothy 2, 3), and even death cannot separate us from the love of God (Romans 8, 38–39). So God will never cease to offer repentance and salvation even to those who reap the consequences of their earthly hatreds and injustices in bodies which suffer torment. What God wills for all is Paradise, and if any do not attain it, it is because of their own hatred, greed, and ignorance.

On such a view, there are many circles of Hell, but it is possible (I do not say inevitable) to move through them, aided by the grace of God in Christ, and finally to enter into a Paradise where an infinity of delights awaits. This final stage was called by Gregory the *apocatastasis*, the regeneration of all things. That could be called a 'new creation'. Just as our physical bodies will be transformed and fulfilled in the possession of spiritual bodies, so this whole physical creation may be transformed and fulfilled in a spiritually infused universe – a different form of universe, but a fulfilment of what was embryonic in this physical universe, and one that brings out all the beauty and goodness that the physical universe has originated and foreshadowed. The writer of 2 Corinthians speaks of our physical body decaying, while our spiritual being is renewed day by day (2 Corinthians 4, 16). It is possible to see this earthly life as a preparation for a future existence in which all pains and sufferings will be ended and all the good things of this world are brought to fulfilment. That final apotheosis of the world will not occur in this universe, or immediately after physical death. It is impossible to assign it to any time in this universe. It is the completion of a long spiritual journey, which begins here and continues in worlds yet to come.

Is all this dreaming and wishful thinking? It is certainly speculation, and involves an appeal to imagination. But for Christians it is founded on the appearance in our world of the resurrected Jesus, on experiences of the Spirit of God which is able to transform us at least in part in this life, and on belief in the primacy of a spiritual reality, God, who has created this universe in order to bring into existence values which are unique and imperishable. The proper realisation of such values seems to require that for vast numbers of

persons who do not realise many of them in this world, there must
be a life beyond the life of this world.[3] A Christian will say that if, in
our lives, we experience something of the loving presence of God
and of the love of Christ who died to liberate us from evil, then we
may hope for such liberation as the proper completion of our lives.
All philosophical reflection can do is try to show that such a hope is
not absurd or impossible and that if there is a cosmic mind who wills
the fullest realisation of personal values, that hope will be vindicated.

[3] Kant said that 'No man can possibly be righteous without having the hope . . . that righteousness must
   have its reward' (*Lectures on Ethics*, 1782, p. 54, trans. Louis Infield, Harper, 1963). Kant's so-called
   'moral argument for God' is often ridiculed as some sort of aberration, but in fact it is central to Kant's
   philosophy that serious commitment to moral action entails the possibility of and the hope for moral
   success.

CHAPTER 18

Moral Demand and Human Fulfilment

The demands of Goodness, I have affirmed, are clear. They require that humans should be creative, appreciative, understanding, cooperative, and compassionate. But these demands are obscured by the hardships which may occur in our lives; by the insensitivity and cruelty of others towards us; by our own tendencies to greed, hatred, and ignorance; and by our uncertainties about whether personal goodness is worth pursuing, or is even possible.

Some people think that moral rules exist mainly for the purpose of keeping social order and maintaining security of personal life and property. Any pursuit of personal fulfilment over and above this is a matter of personal choice, not moral obligation. There is, they think, no one ideal for human life, such as the one I have outlined.

So if anyone chooses to strive for full understanding, appreciation, and sensitivity, great concern for the welfare of others, and maximal creative cooperation with others, that is their personal affair, not a moral matter at all. It may even be thought that such ideal goals are unrealistic and are unlikely to be realised, thus leading to depression and despair. People may think that it is better to aim at a reasonable degree of understanding, concern, and creativity but balance such ideals with a degree of self-interest, competitiveness, and the subjugation of others to one's own will and interests. This seems to be how most nation states and many commercial businesses view their obligations. Personal goodness must be balanced, it is thought, with the demands of personal survival and the interests of one's own family or group. Personal morality should not be so demanding.[1]

Such thoughts can be compounded by a feeling that nature is indifferent to morality. Nature wounds and kills innocent and guilty alike. We should survive as best we can, even if this requires killing, lying, and what might seem, from a strictly impersonal point of view, as injustice. If and when it becomes apparent that other people lie to us, try to dominate us, and are grossly unjust and self-interested, it is even harder to believe that we should not respond in kind – and that if we do not we will almost inevitably lose out in the battle for social pre-eminence and personal security. After all, does anyone really care for the equal welfare of all human beings? Is it not more accurate to say that we care for the welfare of our own family, nation, religion, or race more than we care for those unknown peoples who compete with us for the scarce goods of our world? Thus it is easy to justify giving in to our own greed, hatred, and ignorance, at least to an extent that is not self-defeating, and setting aside the pursuit of seemingly unrealistic ideals which might, in the abstract, seem morally demanding but are in the life of this harsh and competitive world often suicidal.

What this shows is that our views of the nature of the world and our ideas of morality are closely bound together. If we think that a creative mind of supreme beauty and perfection lies at the heart of reality, we will think that every other consideration should take second place to the attempt to achieve union with such a mind. The search for earthly survival and dominance over others, for

---

[1] This is the view that morality should be tailored to basic human self-interest and limited altruism, which are rooted in us by cognitive structures that evolutionary selection has favoured. The biologist and philosopher Michael Ruse, whom I proudly count as a friend, nevertheless shocks me profoundly when he says that in ethics 'we have a collective illusion of the genes' (*Evolutionary Naturalism*, Routledge, 1995), p. 250. If this were true, what could we do with an illusion but dispel it, and seek a less demanding morality, better tailored to our animal natures?

temporary pleasures and soon-to-be-forgotten praise by other men and women, will fade away before the attraction of a Beauty that can never fade or pass into forgetfulness. But if we think that we are accidents in a pointless universe, then personal survival, transient fame, and as much pleasure as this body allows will be all there is.

It is the case, whichever view one takes, that the moral life is one of tension between the ideals of personal fulfilment and the necessities of personal survival in a world of conflict. For all of us, personal ideals must sometimes be compromised by the need to prevent gross injustice. Yet for an idealist the ideals remain in place and have primary importance, because they outline the true goals of human existence.

The idealist view presupposes that there is an objective purpose for human existence, a way in which humans live that fulfils their nature. And each person has a unique personal purpose, arising from the historical and social conditions into which they are born and the temperaments and abilities that they possess. This purpose is to pursue, in many diverse individual forms, the virtues of creativity, appreciation, understanding, synergy, and empathy. In their pursuit lies the fulfilment of personal being, and in their completion lies the realisation of personal happiness.

Many people think that engaging in such a pursuit is its own reward and that it should not need any backup from the long-term prudence of some reward either in this life or after death. In one sense, this is importantly true. One should not pursue the Good just because it pays. But if you put the question 'Why be good?' it is not fully satisfactory to be told that there is no other reason than that one ought to be good, just for its own sake, even if there are no beneficial consequences for anyone. If we come to the conclusion that all our deepest moral beliefs are in the end matters of subjective personal decision or social convention, it may even come to seem irrational that we should commit ourselves to heroic acts that may involve self-sacrifice and death just because we have decided (for no objectively good reason) to do so. We may have the feeling that such a course of action is somehow admirable. But we may equally well have the feeling that it is imprudent and pointless. There is nothing in our world view that makes moral action objectively binding, or especially important for living as a human being (an evolutionary accident, after all).

It is in some such way that the belief in beauty and perfect goodness as lying at the very heart of reality may give a sense of objective truth and moral importance and intensity to our moral endeavours. There really is, in objective reality, a moral purpose for human lives, and there is a way in which humans ought to live. When we act morally, we act in accordance with the true nature of what we are, and we act appropriately in relation to the nature of the universe in which we exist. For many of us, therefore, idealism provides a strong rational basis for moral commitment and action.

It may also seem that since the pursuit of virtue is arduous and often unsuccessful, there is not much hope of the process ever being completed, and of human persons being truly fulfilled. However, idealists believe that the goal and its demands are set by a supreme mind that is able to bring the process to completion. Not only does God set the goals of human endeavour; God also makes it possible for those goals to be achieved, and acts to help in their realisation.

Idealists are not committed to any specific view of how the moral goals of the cosmos will be achieved. Cosmic optimists will think they can be achieved within this universe or even on this planet at some future time. But they may also be achieved beyond this universe, in a life in the world to come. Such a thing is possible because God, a mind who knows all that occurs in the cosmos in a full and perfect way, will retain such knowledge in the divine mind forever. Thus all that finite beings have ever experienced will continue to exist in the mind of God, and they will never be lost. Some philosophers call this 'objective immortality'. I have argued, however, that it is possible that God can re-embody finite persons in ways which enable them to access experiences and also to complete the possibilities in them that were never fully realised during earthly life. It is in this way that the goals of human lives, so frustrated in many lives and partly unachieved in all lives, may finally be achieved.

In each human life there are possibilities of unique creativity. There is something that each person can do that expresses his or her own capacities and interests. But such expression can be frustrated in many ways: by physical disadvantages, by social conditions, by the hostility of other people, or by unwise personal choices – and sometimes by sheer inertia or by positively destructive elements of character. Some of these frustrations can be partly removed by loving friendship and by personal character formation, yet it is perhaps rare that a person's potential creativity can find full and appropriate expression. As Aristotle said, true happiness, which lies in the free expression of human excellence, is attained by few, and then infrequently and only for a while. That is a rather pessimistic thought, but it all too often describes the human situation quite well.

Much the same is true of the human capacities to appreciate beauty and understand the intelligibility and intricacy of the cosmos. In most of us they lie largely undeveloped and blunted by a sense of the boredom of the habitual and a rejection of persistent intellectual effort. Thus, that which we have it in us to be remains potential, and what we all are, to some degree, is a shadow of what we could be.

Not only are our capacities limited and frustrated. Human experiences, too, remain largely insubstantial and incomplete. We are barely conscious of many things we experience; we forget much of the past, and invent much of it; we fail to integrate our experiences properly, so as to apply what we have learned to present experience; and we fail to foresee the outcomes of the things we set our minds on.

God, having knowledge of all things, takes into the divine being all those imperfect and frustrated capacities and experiences. Although they may be imperfect, they are nevertheless genuinely new experiences, and they incorporate many worthwhile states that otherwise would never have existed. To that extent they add to God's actual knowledge.

Still, though God's knowledge is perfect, we do not want to think of God actually feeling all the frustrations and sufferings that finite creatures undergo, just in the way that creatures do. Indeed, such a thing seems not to be possible, since part of creaturely suffering is sometimes the feeling that pain fills the whole of one's experience or that life itself is pointless and depressing. Further, many human experiences, for instance those of mass murderers, are intrinsically evil. Such experiences can never be experienced by God in that form. God must know that they occur and must know what they are like. But God will never actually experience that life is pointless, and God must condemn experiences that are intrinsically evil. So there must be a certain 'distancing' of God from human experiences as we undergo them.

We must conclude that all human experiences will affect the divine experience and cause God to feel either empathy or condemnation, which would not exist in God without the occurrence of finite experiences. But human experiences as such cannot be the actual experiences of God.

For instance, God knows that we suffer and what it is like for us to suffer. But God also knows that our sufferings can in some way and at some time be subsumed within a greater whole in which we will find an overwhelming happiness. A very remote analogy might be comprehended by thinking of a hard, even tragic, journey towards a very worthwhile goal – perhaps when someone climbs Everest without oxygen. That person may later remember (know) the difficult episodes, but now see how those are parts of a whole pattern which was part of achieving a worthwhile goal. Knowledge of happiness obtained through struggle is different from knowledge of just pure happiness. It involves knowing the difficult parts but seeing them as 'overcome' and as having helped make us what we are even though we could not have desired them for their own sakes.

So in God there may be gradations of knowledge, of intensity of feeling and regard, and each part must be seen within a developing totality, which is overall of great worth. Our sufferings and our evil inclinations, as well as our happiness and our virtues, will always be known by and exist within the mind of God. But in God they will always be associated with divine responses of either condemnation or approval. A supremely good God would desire that evil and suffering cease to exist and that virtue and happiness be completed and fully realised. It is in the context of such a perspective – where evil is to be overcome and goodness is to be fulfilled, and where the whole life of the world is placed within a wider totality of divine experience and knowledge – that God experiences the lives of finite persons. That divine experience – the experience of Absolute Spirit, in idealist terms – may then be accessed in appropriate ways by persons if they continue to exist beyond this earthly life.

Thus it is possible that human sufferings may be capable of incorporation into a greater worthwhile totality in which evil is finally eliminated and new forms of goodness, forged out of often ambiguous and frustrated human experiences, will be brought to perfection. This means that it is not enough that God can know, approve of, or condemn the experiences of finite creatures. The experiences of those creatures must be capable of being either brought to fulfilment or to judgment. If the demands of morality are real and pressing, then we might expect that, in a rationally and morally ordered universe, both judgment and fulfilment must also be real.

Christians believe that all that we do in this life will be subject to divine judgment and that we shall eventually reap the just consequences of our actions and thoughts. The afterlife will not just be a new sort of life which we could have experienced even if we had never existed in this universe. It will be a world in which the consequences of our life in this world will be justly worked out. This may be a rather fearful prospect if we just consider our very imperfect natures. But if God truly cares for our good, we may hope that God will lead us, perhaps through successive stages, to the full realisation of our natures and to conscious relation to the Supreme Good.[2] It will always be possible for us to turn from evil and be led towards the good. This hope is not a hope for 'pie in the sky when we die', which has no implications for our moral and social lives in this world. It is the realisation that what we do in this world is of immense importance, because it will determine what our existence in the world to come may be.

---

[2] This is the picture of the afterlife which is affirmed by the fourth-century St. Gregory of Nyssa, in his treatise *On the Soul and Resurrection*: 'When from the nutritive part within them [human souls] everything that is the reverse or the counterfeit of it has been picked out, and has been committed to the fire that consumes everything unnatural, and so has disappeared, then ... their humanity will thrive ... and some day after long courses of ages will get back again that universal form which God stamped upon us at the beginning' (in *The Nicene and Post-Nicene Fathers*, vol. 5, trans. A. H. Wilson, T and T Clark, 1988) p. 468.

CHAPTER 19

Judgment and Compassion

I have spoken of judgment. Can anything be said philosophically about the nature of divine judgment? I suppose that for many people the idea of a judgment after death is some sort of fantasy. Death may be the end, and any sort of moral judgment there may be has to be seen in this one life. I understand that attitude, and I think one can go some way towards saying that there is a sort of moral judgment in this life. As Plato argued, those who choose evil demean their humanity and fail to find happiness and fulfilment.[1] Those who choose the good find the life of virtue to be its own fulfilment. I believe this to be true, but only in general and for the most part. In many cases, the evil flourish and the good suffer oppression and misery. The claims of goodness may remain imperative in this world, even if this life is all there is. But I find it hard to see why one should believe in moral imperatives if one sees human existence itself as a brief cosmic accident. And I think that those who hold such views simply have to adopt the heroic stance that they should seek what is good despite realising the probability of failure and of personal suffering. Then I wonder why I think that such an attitude is 'heroic' when it may rather seem to be irrational. I do want to say, with atheists, that morality does exercise a categorical claim over our lives.

---

[1] Plato, *The Republic*. The opening argument with Thrasymachus is a classic text.

Maybe for atheists that is absurd,[2] but I have the irrepressible feeling that it is right.

For an idealist philosophy, however, that sense of categorical obligation is a sign of something objective and real and of decisive importance in revealing what human existence is. The universe may seem to be indifferent to morality and to the moral ideals and hopes of humanity. But the insufficiency of a purely material universe to make intelligible the highest moral aims of humanity may also point to the fact that the material universe is not all there is.[3] An idealist will already have come to the view that conscious experiences and the existence of responsible subject-selves are not reducible to or explicable in terms of a purely materialist philosophy (as argued in Part I). The idealist philosopher will think that there is a coherent concept of one supreme mind as the source of material reality and that this provides an intelligible explanation of the existence of the universe in terms of intrinsic and objective value (as argued in Part II). The idealist is therefore prepared to see the existence of objective and categorical moral obligations as rooted in the nature of that supreme mind. This will not be a wish-fulfilling fantasy, but rather part of a rational assessment of the ultimate nature of the reality of which humans are part. The sense of moral obligation is the most important part of such a world view as far as practical life is concerned, and the idealist would hope that such a sense would remain – as it does in contemporary Western humanism – even if the world view is rejected. Nevertheless, the idealist will affirm that the thought of a moral order to the universe is a just and accurate perception of the spiritual nature of things. And if there is such a moral order, then the moral lives of humans will be subject to

---

[2] Camus, in his novel *The Plague*, expounds the view that moral commitment is obligatory, though it is absurd in a world without objective meaning or justice.

[3] Cf. Immanuel Kant, who writes of 'a feeling of the insufficiency of the contingent for realising the moral destination of human existence' (*Religion within the Limits of Reason Alone*, 1794, book 3).

judgment by the supreme mind which is the source of all legitimate moral demands. That judgment will, however, have to occur after earthly life is over, for it assuredly does not occur in this sublunary world. Thus personal idealists will very naturally be committed to the thought of a trans-world judgment.

Obviously, as I have conceded, large elements of imagination will be involved in any speculation about what an afterlife will be like. And it would be disingenuous of me to pretend that the Christian tradition (in large part shared by Jews, Muslims, and many Hindus) has played no part in my speculations. Yet my chief concern is to see, by the use of a thought experiment, what a morally just judgment could be like, from a philosophical point of view.

For an idealist, it is important to see that any final judgment will be made by a being of supreme goodness. In the light of an analysis of goodness such as I have suggested in this part, it will be clear that such a being will never cause harm for its own sake. It will never be vindictive or vengeful. It will always desire the welfare of others.

Yet humans often cause great harm to others and to themselves – through hatred, greed, and ignorance. They thereby become unfitted for participation in a communion of love. They descend into a world of violence and conflict. In this life, this may be concealed, as the unjust flourish and the humble are oppressed. In the world to come, if that world is morally ordered, the deep consequences of hatred will be unveiled, as persons who have hated others become themselves imprisoned in a world of ceaseless war of all against all. In this life there is no sharp division between those who instigate war and those who desire peace. Those who suffer conflict are often, even usually, not those who will or deserve it. In the world to come those who instigate conflict suffer it and those who desire peace obtain it.

Judgment is the division of the world of war and egoism from the world of peace and self-giving. The division is not absolute and unbridgeable. It is possible to turn from greed to sympathy for others, and even in a peaceful world there is still much to learn and many virtues yet to pursue.

Continuing with thought experiments about what an afterlife might be like where perfect justice is realised, we may suppose that after this life each will go to a place in the afterworld for which they have fitted themselves. They will come to know themselves as they truly are, and they will reap what they have sown.[4] It may not be a realm of strict retribution, where there is a fixed and unalterable penalty or reward for every responsible act. But it will be a realm where what one experiences is the result of what one has thought and done, for good or ill.

It is not fitting to think of such judgment as the imposition of a punishment by an angry God. As Plato said, a just man will never cause harm,[5] and so a just God will never cause harm unless it is intended to lead to good. Medieval pictures of tortures in Hell are unacceptably vindictive, because torturing anyone is wrong, no matter how much harm the victims have caused. But malignant souls cannot be admitted to perfect happiness, and so they do forfeit many goods, and especially the greatest good of sharing in the being of Goodness itself. Moreover, if their lives have been filled with hatred, envy, malice, and greed, they have made themselves unable to respond to love, humility, sympathy, and benevolence.

In an existence in which hatred and greed are no longer concealed by convention or hypocrisy, those dispositions will become self-destructive. What has been called 'Hell' (not a word, incidentally,

---

[4] See the Biblical picture of a division into 'wheat' and 'tares', in (e.g.) Matthew 13, 24–30. Though clearly metaphorical, this does entail a division of good and evil.

[5] Plato, *The Republic*, opening argument with Polemarchus.

that appears in the Bible) is not a fixed penalty imposed from without by a ruthless God. Even less is it endless and inescapable torment for a finite lifetime of evildoing. It is the complete rule of hatred, greed, and ignorance in a world which the evil have fashioned for themselves, and in which they are able to continually harm each other and themselves.[6] Such places exist in this life, in the many wars and tyrannies that occur. But in the world to come, a world where true justice reigns, the innocent are delivered from suffering, and evil and suffering are inexorably tied together.

A supremely good God, to continue the thought experiment, would not be content to leave this situation untouched. It may be that for some, destruction becomes total. A life fixed immovably in hatred, a life shut out from the presence of God, who is the source of all being, will in the end simply cease to be. For evil and suffering cannot remain in being forever. Such negativity must end in complete negation of being.

But there is a better alternative. Hatred and greed may come to recognise their true nature, and pity for oneself may open the way to sympathy for others. Souls in Hell may not entirely lose the capacity for pity and sympathy. So, by effort and discipline, and a growing desire for a dimly recognised good, they may ascend to realms where evil is diminished and the suffering associated with it begins to fade. It is not that the price of evil has been paid – as if there was such a definite price that could be paid – but that as selfish and vindictive tendencies lessen, the virtues of friendship and concern for others begin to grow. The grip of evil is lessened, and glimpses of love and happiness begin to transform selves which have been bound to evil by long habituation. And we might think

---

[6] One of the best imaginative descriptions of Hell is in Jean-Paul Sartre's play *Huis Clos* ('No Exit'), in which occurs the phrase 'Hell is other people' – and, one might add, Hell is also living with the self that one has become through one's sadomasochistic relation to others.

that Goodness itself would play a positive part, as it helps transform the habits of the self-imprisoned soul and fit it for wider and fuller forms of existence.[7]

Thus we may think, with Gregory of Nyssa, of many levels of the world to come, from the deepest depravity to the highest beatitude. Each of us will find a level appropriate to what we have responsibly made of our earthly lives. But those levels are not fixed unchangeably and forever. Attracted by the light of the Supreme Good, we can ascend through many forms of being. As we ascend, our evil dispositions will weaken, and our sufferings will diminish. That is, we may think, what a supremely good and non-vindictive God would desire and make possible.

Some have spoken of the 'fear of Hell' as a major motivation of the moral life. This cannot, however, be fear of endless torment by malignant demons or by a ruthless God, as a punishment for a set of specific 'sins' which we may have committed. It must be a discernment of the sort of existence that our own dispositions, reinforced by habit, are leading us towards. It must be recognition that hatred, fear, and ignorance will lead to the destruction of our personalities and to increased pain and suffering. And it must include a faith that even the depths of self-destruction are not excluded from the presence and attraction of the Good. So it must include a desire that God can somehow enable us to overcome our self-destructive habits and be transformed by the power of goodness. It must include the resolution to counter hatred, fear, and ignorance by attention to the Good and reliance on its power to heal and transfigure our lives. Then the 'fear of Hell' — now seen as the recognition of our self-destructive tendencies and the possibility and necessity of turning our minds to attend to the Good — can be

---

[7] This is a view expounded in John Hick's classic work *Death and Eternal Life* (Macmillan, 1976).

an incentive to change the course of our lives and seek what is truly good both for others and for ourselves.

Philosophical reflection on what just judgment by a supremely good God might be can lead thus far. But at this point a consideration that derives mostly from the Christian faith adds another dimension to such reflection. It is one that sometimes seems strange even to adherents of other monotheistic faiths. It is the idea of divine self-sacrifice. Such divine sacrifice can, however, be seen as the ultimate and definitive form of divine compassion, and thus as part of divine perfection. While it is based on specifically Christian insights, it may become accepted as a natural and reflective philosophical insight into the nature of divine compassion.

Divine self-sacrifice for the sake of qualifying strict divine judgment is not just an overlooking or forgetting of the evil that creatures do. It is not a repudiation of just judgment. It is a positive self-renouncing action to share in the despair and desolation that evil brings about, and by that sharing to begin to overcome it by the persuasive power of unceasing and invincible love. It is by such sacrifice that the greatest compassion is shown without repudiating recognition of the seriousness of judgment.

Even beings which have devoted themselves to hatred and evil are not left alone and without hope. There is a divine presence that enters into their wretched state of existence, and by doing so opens up for them a path to liberation and new life. 'If I make my bed in *Sheol*, you are there' (Psalm 139, verse 8). Divine self-sacrifice is the highest form of unlimited compassion.

The idea of sacrifice itself is common to many religions, and it was central to the ancient Hebrew religion. It is natural to pray to whatever spiritual beings there may be for help and to offer them some symbol of devotion and commitment. It may be flowers, food, or incense, or it may be the life of a valued animal. In the Old

Testament we find references to the practice of sacrificing firstborn sons to the gods, and the story of Abraham and Isaac possibly marks a time when such a practice was not unknown in ancient Israel and when God was believed to have provided a ram for sacrifice instead, marking the end of child sacrifice in Israel.

The common element of sacrifice is the giving up of something of great value. This may be seen as a gift to persuade a god to help (*do ut des*) or – more insightfully – as a costly token of personal commitment to and self-abandoning dependence upon God. In the Hebrew Bible the idea of sacrifice as an atonement for sin is prevalent, though it should be noted that there was no atonement for sin 'with a high hand' – intentional, conscious evildoing.[8] In general, sacrifice was an expression of contrition, and the giving up was a sign of the desire to make amends, a sign of the genuineness of one's desire to accept a voluntary sacrifice to try to bring good out of evil by aligning oneself with the will of God. In the Old Testament sacrifices there is also an element of sharing a fellowship meal with God, so that it was not just a gift in the hope of obtaining future favours, but also the expression of a desire to share in communion with God.

So the notion of humans sacrificing to God was widespread in the ancient world, and the sacrificial ritual was a complex one carrying connotations of devotion, loyalty, gratitude, contrition, and desire for fellowship with the divine. What is not so common is the idea that the divine life is also characterised by sacrifice – the sacrifice of divine beatitude and beauty by an entrance into a world of hatred, egoism, and despair. Such an idea was 'foolishness to the Greeks',[9] who placed the divine far above and untouched by the terrors of the temporal world. Even in some Hindu cosmologies, when the gods enter into time as avatars, they do so as beings who

---

[8] See Numbers 15, 30–31.   [9] 1 Corinthians 1, 22–26.

retain their omnipotence and omniscience, who do not feel the pains and agonies of the world.

This is very different from the Christian belief that God suffered and died, being treated as a criminal and subjected to the scorn and derision of men and women. The theology of the cross may seem to be totally at odds with a rational theism that sees God as the unchanging and unchanged creator of all worlds, unable to share in or even fully relate to sublunary beings immersed in a world of time and change.

Yet the philosophy of personal idealism may suggest a rather different picture of God. I think that one insight of that annoyingly obscure philosopher Hegel that is worth pondering is his transformation of the idea of divine infinity.

In ancient philosophy, infinity was often regarded as a defect – for everything real had to have definite, and therefore limited, dimensions. However, as Christian philosophy developed, it came to be thought that God, as creator of all, must be beyond all limited and created beings and to be infinite in being unbounded by any other reality at all. So in Aquinas, God's infinity excludes everything finite, for the finite would be a form of limitation. The infinite is not another being in addition to the finite, for it is not in the same dimension of being at all. The infinite is the absolutely unbounded, and nothing finite can exist within it. So Aquinas says, astonishingly, that God has no real relation to creation; that is, God remains unchanged by anything that exists in time.[10]

This is astonishing because for Christians Jesus is precisely God embodied in time. But Aquinas had very sophisticated ways of

---

[10] Aquinas, *Summa Theologiae*, question 6, article 2: 'The relations that God is said to bear to creatures . . . really exist not in God but in the creatures'. In other words, God is not changed by anything that happens in the universe. In my view, this is true of God's eternal and necessary nature, yet there are necessarily contingent aspects of the divine nature, and these change as they relate to changes in creatures.

construing divine incarnation. In short, all the changes that occurred at the incarnation were changes in human or physical nature, and not changes in God. This is very helpful in countering unduly anthropomorphic ideas of God and in entailing that no easy or literal account of incarnation will be adequate. God did not 'become' human and did not walk around in Galilee, except in the sense that the human Jesus, being uniquely and ineffably united to God, could correctly be called 'God walking, eating, suffering, and dying' – but the divine nature itself did not do such things. Thus a gap is opened up between the human and divine natures in Jesus, the temporal and changing, and the eternal and changeless. Whatever sort of 'identity' there is between the changeless and the changing, it is not of any simple sort. That, of course, is all to the good. But it does seem strange that human and divine form one 'person',[11] while yet the divine does not really share most of the properties of the human, and in particular its sufferings, development, and human personal relationships.

The Hegelian transformation of the idea of infinity was to say that the infinite does not exclude the finite but must include everything, since it is bounded by nothing. So all time must be included in, not excluded from, the infinite. This led, in Hegel, to absolute idealism, the view that the absolute consists of everything, which develops itself historically in time but is in itself beyond all times. But it also gave rise, in a more overtly theistic form of belief, to the view that God does not exclude the temporal, but must include it, and perhaps relate to temporal things in new and responsive ways. This view is prominently stated in modern times by Karl Barth, though Barth affirms the same paradox as Hegel, that God (the

---

[11] The definition of the Council of Chalcedon (451 AD) defined Jesus as having two 'natures' (divine and human) in one 'person'. A major implication of this is that Jesus was truly human, with all the limitations that entails, as well as being one (in some sense) with the divine.

absolute – in Hegel, of course) is in time but is also timeless.[12] I think this paradox stands in need of, and is capable of, clarification.

There is no contradiction in the view that a creator of a universe could, in principle, have the power to take form within that universe and play a part in the reality which the creator had brought about. Of course such a creator would remain in its transcendent reality but could add to it a temporal agency. That seems to be the traditional Christian view, for which Jesus is the temporal image of the creator.

The clarification that I think is needed is to say that the addition of a temporal image to God does change God, and thus qualifies an Aristotelian or Thomist account. Such an addition also means that God is in a real sense complex, consisting of both timeless and temporal properties. It is important that these properties do not contradict, and so God cannot be temporal and timeless in the same respects. As I argued in Chapter 14, God will be timeless and necessary in the divine existence and nature – being supremely powerful, knowing, and loving. But God will be temporal and contingent in acting contingently to express the divine nature – in doing, knowing, and relating affectively to temporal and contingent things.

This can already be seen as a form of divine self-sacrifice. For relation to and sharing in the life of temporal being involves suffering and death. However, it is not all sacrifice, since it also makes possible mutual creativity and loving relationship to beings who are other than God.

Human lives, however, have become subject to hatred, greed, and egoism, which have become implanted in human nature over many generations. For God to take form in such a world involves sacrifice in a deeper way. For it entails subjecting the divine life to

[12] Karl Barth, *Church Dogmatics*, ed. G. W. Bromiley and T. F. Torrance (T and T Clark, 1937) ii/2, p. 110: 'Time is not excluded from his [God's] duration but included in it.'

the hatred, greed, and egoism of estranged finite persons. Divine power could, no doubt, easily have defeated any such hostility. But divine love seeks to transform hatred, greed, and egoism into love, compassion, and beneficence.

It does so, the life of Jesus suggests, by 'bearing our sins'[13] – that is, by a life of compassion, beneficence, and reconciliation that refuses to accept the values and habits of an estranged world and that as a result suffers the worst that such alleged values can do.

The central Christian symbols of crucifixion and resurrection show that resolute love in an estranged world can lead to suffering and death. But they also show that love is stronger than death, and in being resurrected from death Jesus showed that the way of transformation from spiritual death to spiritual ('eternal') life is always open for those who follow him. And, since he offers his life for all people without exception, it is possible for all without exception to follow him in that way.

The self-sacrifice of God is, then, the divine sharing in the estranged condition of humanity. Suffering, as human, a cruel death is the result of human evil. God's self-sacrifice is a gift of the divine life to human persons; it is a sharing in human suffering and death; it is, in the person of Jesus, a making-one of divine and human; and it is a way of bringing all human beings to share in the divine life.[14]

---

[13] 'He himself bore our sins in his body on the cross, so that, free from sins, we might live for righteousness' (1 Peter 2, 24).

[14] In *Christ and the Cosmos* I have treated the doctrines of the Trinity and Incarnation. It may be thought that I am saying little about the third great distinctive Christian doctrine, the Atonement. That is because what I believe about this has been well said in two magnificent books by Paul Fiddes, *The Creative Suffering of God* (Clarendon, 1988) and *Past Event and Present Salvation* (Darton, Longman, Todd, 1989). For my relatively minor points of disagreement with Prof. Fiddes, see 'Freedom, Necessity and Suffering in God', in *Within the Love of God*, ed. Anthony Clarke and Andrew Moore (Oxford University Press, 2014). I also have a short passage in *Morality, Autonomy, and God* (Oneworld, 2013), pp. 204–206, where I sketch what may be called a 'participatory' account of atonement, one that stresses the self-sacrificial grace of Christ that enables us to participate, through him and in the power of the Spirit, in the divine life.

A personal idealist who is a Christian can therefore say that the divine nature is personal in the profound sense that it can truly be expressed in a finite person. Judgment is real, for evil carries the ultimate consequence of self-destruction. But the Christian Gospel – the good news – is that no one has to be trapped in evil forever. God has come where humans are and shared their estranged way of being. The divine life delivers them from the ultimate consequence of their own evil. For God gives the divine life to humans that humans might share in it.[15] God has, one might say, undergone the judgment that is proper to humans, in order to offer to humanity a way of liberation.

Of course humans still have to learn to overcome self and deny evil, and the way may seem hard and long. But persons no longer do this in their own strength. They do it in the strength of the Lord, who has died to free them from ultimate judgment and who rose from death to give them 'life more abounding'.

This does seem like the supreme possibility of goodness for a personal God who created finite persons so that they might share in eternal life, who sees human persons turning away from goodness, and who goes to the furthest possible lengths to help them turn back, without overruling their freedom. That furthest length is a life of self-giving love that is not defeated by death and that can give its strength to all who will accept it.

I am not suggesting that philosophy alone can lead us to this point. I am suggesting that in the Christian Gospel we can see a consummation, and not a contradiction, of personal idealism. In this sense, Christian faith does not contradict reason. It shows where reason at its best leads. If this was foolishness to the

---

[15] Athanasius, 'God became man that man might become God' (*On the Incarnation*, sec. 54). This often-quoted phrase is frequently used by celebrating priests at the Holy Eucharist.

Greeks, it was because the Greeks, for all their wisdom, did not have a clear idea of what a truly personal mind of the cosmos could be. They could not envisage the passion of God, the love of God for the world, and the possibility that the material world itself might become capable of expressing the Divine purpose and nature.

CHAPTER 20

Kenosis and Theosis

In accordance with the philosophy of personal idealism, I have developed a notion of God as a passionate mind who sacrifices divine beatitude in order to relate to created minds. This has sometimes been called a kenotic concept of God. The theology of *kenosis* is associated primarily with the work of some Lutheran theologians in Germany and with Charles Gore in England.[1] It posed a radical challenge to the traditional notion of God, which had been developed by a long line of Christian theologians, most notably perhaps Augustine, Anselm, and Aquinas.

That traditional notion is that God is eternal, in the sense of being timeless – that is, without temporal relation to anything in time and without internal relations of a temporal nature. God is necessary, so that God has to be what God is and could not possibly be otherwise. God is also simple, in that there are no different properties in God which can combine to produce the divine being. Rather, all properties in God coincide in such a way that there is no inner complexity in God at all. As Aquinas put it, the existence of God is identical with the divine essence.[2] So if God is timeless and necessary, then God is totally timeless and necessary in every respect.

---

[1] Some of the material in this chapter is based on my paper 'Cosmos and Kenosis', in *The Work of Love*, ed. John Polkinghorne (SPCK, 2001).

[2] Aquinas, *Summa Theologiae* 1a, question 3, article 3.

It follows from this that God is strictly immutable. Whatever happens in the created cosmos makes no difference to God and does not change God in any way. The cosmos is created in a non-temporal act, and God creates every moment of time, from first to last, in one and the same act of intentional causation. An important implication of this view is that temporal events such as the incarnation cause no change in the nature of God. The incarnation is part of the one creative divine act and thus may rightly be said to have been willed from the beginning of creation. The crucifixion caused no change in God, and while the human nature of Jesus suffers, the divine nature does not.

The nineteenth-century Lutheran idea of *kenosis*, which has its roots in some of the writings of Luther but develops them in a new way, radically challenged this traditional account. Basing their theology of incarnation on Philippians 2, 7 ('Christ Jesus, though he was in the form of God … emptied himself, taking the form of a servant'), kenotic theologians held that the incarnation brought about a radical change in the eternal Word. The Word, being in the form of God, is properly omnipotent and omniscient. When the Word becomes flesh, however, he empties himself of some of these divine attributes. Generally speaking, when the Word takes the form of a man, he gives up omnipotence and omniscience. He either actually renounces those divine properties or he refrains from employing them (Lutheran theologians disagreed about the most appropriate description).

So it was held that if God is truly to become man, God must set aside or radically curtail the divine properties. Such properties are retained, however, by the Father and by the Holy Spirit and can be restored to Christ at the proper time. Such a kenotic view entails that there is change in God, and therefore that there is time – understood, as in Aristotle, as the 'measure of change' – in

God. If the Word really became a human being, it also entails that there is suffering in God, so that God is passible, changed by what happens in the created cosmos.

Why did the Lutheran theologians make this change in the concept of God? Part of the impetus for a kenotic Christology lies in the desire to preserve the sense that God enters fully into the human situation, understands it from the inside, and shares the human condition. Many Christians feel that if a changeless God simply assumes a human nature to the divine nature, the sense in which God shares in human suffering is purely verbal and that something of the pathos and depth of the incarnation is lost. Luther's strong sense of the importance of the passion and the cross in Christianity led him to an insistence that the divine nature of the Word must truly share in suffering and thus enter fully into the human situation.

Another reason for adopting a kenotic Christology is, to put it in the broadest theological terms, the rejection of either a Platonic or an Aristotelian concept of God (Luther called Aristotle 'that buffoon who has misled the Church'). In such philosophies the timeless is superior to the temporal, the changeless is superior to the changing, and the intelligible and universal is superior to the material and particular. So the supreme reality, God, is seen as timeless, changeless, and universal (a subsistent Form).

Since about the sixteenth century, however, and the rise of the natural sciences, the material and particular have been seen as the truly 'real', while the universal has come to seem an abstraction. Time and change, aspects of the material, become important aspects of reality, not simply illusory or merely apparent. The Reformed tendency to give Scripture a more literal interpretation also contributed to the idea that the God of Abraham, Isaac, and Jacob is a dynamic and creative being who interacts with humans and who even changes the divine mind after conversations with Moses or Abraham. However mysterious the inner reality of God may be (God is still hidden in the 'cloud of un-knowing'), it does seem that this God enters into time and change, and is in responsive relationship with human persons.[3]

Though the kenotic theory arose through reflection on what it means for God to be incarnate in Jesus, one might well think that the divine sharing in finite experience and action cannot be confined to just one case on the planet earth. God must share in all finite experience, wherever in the universe it is. God must truly feel, by a direct and empathetic form of apprehension, every experience that creatures have. That may give a deeper view of divine omniscience: not merely a factual registering by God that something is the case, but God's acquaintance with what each experience is like.

This means that God relates to finite creatures in ways which make the divine reality different than it would have been had there been no such creatures. For such a more relational or participative view of God, it would be an imperfection not to know affectively what creaturely experiences are like. Any being that coexists with suffering creatures would be less perfect if it failed to have affective knowledge of what those creatures experience.

If one takes that seriously, then one may say that not just the incarnation, but also the creation of conscious and rational beings itself is a kenotic act on God's part. For it will involve a giving up of pure divine bliss and accepting many experiences of pain and suffering. It will involve a giving up of complete control and accepting the freedom of created beings to make their own decisions, however misdirected and unwise. It will involve giving up complete knowledge and accepting that much about the future must

---

[3] A fuller exposition of this notable change in outlook is detailed in my *Rational Theology and the Creativity of God* (Blackwell, 1982).

be unknown until it is determined by the actions of creatures. These are real limitations, and this may be thought of as a sort of *kenosis*, a giving up of some great goods in order that free creatures may exist in independence, community, and creativity.

This is not, however, *kenosis* in the sense of giving up divine properties in order just to allow others to possess the values of freedom and community. It is also a way of adding new and distinctive values to the divine being itself. For the creation of finite agents with a real degree of autonomy adds to the divine being the possibility of cooperating with them in creative action, of appreciating their existence and the values they bring into being, and of bringing the cosmic process to a final consummation in which all the values it has brought forth in the long course of its existence will be conserved and apprehended in God forever.

In other words, this sort of *kenosis* is not just a self-giving. It is also and equally importantly a self-realisation, a way in which God realises possibilities that are eternally present in the divine being and comes to experience new forms of value that otherwise would never have been actualised. When God gives up pure bliss, God obtains in return many new sorts of values that could only be actualised in a cosmic process from which finite agents emerge. Of course, these values are mixed with many sorts of disvalues, and necessarily so. Along with the values finite agents create are all the forms of suffering they endure and bring upon each other. Along with the positive cooperation God can experience with finite agents are the many forms of obstruction to the divine will that such agents realise. Along with new creativity go possibilities for destruction and conflict within the cosmos. Nevertheless, theists are committed to believing that the good will far outweigh the bad and that the bad can itself in some way be redeemed, both in the experience of God and, ultimately, for the creatures whom God can unite to the divine experience.

God, on this view, does not just limit the divine being in order that free finite agents might exist. God realises, makes actual, aspects of the divine being that otherwise would have remained potential. Entering into relationship and communion and cooperating in realising new forms of finite value are realisations of great values in and for the divine nature itself. Perhaps some such realisation is essential to the divine nature, so that God necessarily creates other personal agents (though not necessarily these specific personal agents). If one thinks that 'God is love' (1 John 4, 16), that love is an essential property of the divine nature, and that love can only be properly exercised in relation to others who are free to reciprocate love or not, then the creation of some universe containing free finite agents seems to be an implication of the divine nature. However, trying to say what is or is not essential to the divine nature is a presumptuous exercise, and perhaps the most one can do here is to draw attention to a range of implications that follow from various interpretations of the idea of God.

For Christians, this is not simply a piece of abstract metaphysics. It is also a view based firmly on the revelation of the nature of God in the person of Jesus. Philosophy can lead one in the direction of positing a supreme mind which renounces eternal bliss in order to share in the lives of estranged creatures and seeks to reunite those creatures to itself in a renewed and transformed creation. For those who believe that in and through the person of Jesus a revolutionary picture of God as the loving saviour of all humanity was disclosed, this picture provides a clarification, extension, and confirmation of the philosophical speculation. It is a clarification because there is an independent and experiential route to God which converges on what speculative human thought can suggest. It is an extension because the full extent of divine self-giving, the way in which human and divine can be united, and the form of the final union of finite and infinite is revealed. And it is a confirmation because for those who accept the testimony to Jesus' life, death, and resurrection, a philosophical theory is given instantiation in specific events in space and time.

The life of Jesus is important not because it is the only place in the whole of creation where God shows the divine nature as self-giving love. The life of Jesus is important because at one particular time and space it decisively shows what God is, always and everywhere. This is not the only place where God acts in persuasive, self-giving love to draw creatures to the divine. It is the place where God's universal salvific action is expressed and disclosed in a paradigmatic way to human beings.

In Jesus there can be seen a threefold manifestation of the nature and activity of God in relation to the created universe. The first moment of this divine activity is *kenosis*, the self-limiting expression of divine power that brings it into relation with a universe containing finite moral agents. In this relation, God does not order all things by divine fiat, but rather seeks to help and empower moral agents to formulate and attain their own objectives, insofar as they promise to realise good. This means that God will have affective knowledge of forms of suffering and evil, which constitutes a real renunciation of unmixed divine bliss. It means that God will constitute the divine being in relation to others who may to some extent frustrate the divine will. This is a real form of self-limitation, even though it is a true expression and self-manifestation of the divine nature as self-giving love, not a renunciation of that nature.

Jesus' life of healing the sick, forgiving the guilt-ridden, befriending social outcasts, and undermining hypocrisy is a very good image of the compassionate and persuasive love of God.

Because of this disclosure, God can be worshipped not only as the all-powerful source and sustainer of all being, but also as a Father (or indeed a Mother) who cares for finite persons as for children and wishes them to become fully conscious of the divine loving presence. In the moment of *kenosis*, God relates the divine being to creatures who have a proper autonomy and otherness which it is the divine will not to infringe.

The second moment of the divine relation to the cosmos is that of *henosis* (unity), a mysterious but intimate uniting of divine personhood and finite personhood, so that finite lives can become true images of the divine nature and mediators of divine power and so that the divine and many creaturely persons become one. It is through the activity of the Holy Spirit that God acts on this planet within human persons to transform them into transparent images and effective instruments of the divine being. In this relation, creatures do not remain as beings separate and distinct from their heavenly Father, however closely related to him they are in love and respect. Their lives are interpenetrated by the divine Spirit, so that they may, at their best, say with St. Paul, 'Not I live, but Christ lives in me' (Galatians 2, 20).

The inward unity between divine and human was, Christians believe, fully realised in the life of Jesus, but it is part of Christian faith to hope that it will be partly realised, at least, in the lives of all believers. For orthodox Christianity, Jesus was unique in that his humanity was, from the first moment of his existence, inseparably united to the divine Word or Wisdom of God. That eternal Word, inwardly and necessarily unfolded from the being of the primordial creative source of all ('only-begotten of the Father'), was so united to the human person of Jesus that they form one being. The Word (or *Logos*) is, in the language of the Nicene Creed, of 'one substance' with the Father and so is 'very God from very God'. It is one particular form (*hypostasis*) of the one supreme personal God.

It is united to Jesus so that the Word shapes his human life without undermining his human creativity, knowledge, and power and his life mediates the presence and love of God as fully as it can be mediated in human form.

This terminology may seem different from the classical picture of the eternal Word of God, a distinct personal consciousness, 'taking on' the properties of human nature, which is one widespread understanding of Christian theology. But that picture neglects the fact that on the classical view the Word is completely changeless and simple and so does not 'take on' or add to itself anything finite. So the classical view too must speak in terms of a 'union' of human and divine rather than of a strict identity between them. On the picture I am presenting, the Word is a form of being of the one divine consciousness (as are the two other 'forms' of the Trinitarian God: the primordial source – the Father – and the uniting Spirit), not a distinct individual consciousness, and it really changes when it founds a union of human and divine.[4] The picture differs from the classical picture in asserting the radically creative and relational nature of God, and also in asserting that the possession of a real creative subject-agency (but not 'sinfulness', the tendency to frustrate the divine will, a tendency which will presumably be overcome by all humans in the life of the world to come) is an essential part of human nature. But I think that this idealist picture is wholly compatible with Christian creedal orthodoxy, in asserting the full humanity and deity of Jesus Christ and in affirming that God is three *hypostases* in one *ousia*. And it implies more clearly that a unity of humanity and divinity is something that is a goal and a possibility of every finite personal life.

---

[4] This view of the Trinity and of the incarnation of the Word in Jesus is more fully outlined in my *Christ and the Cosmos* (Cambridge University Press, 2016). Excellent critical discussions of this book, and my responses to them, can be found in the journal *Philosophia Christi* (vol. 17, issue 3; November, 2016).

God not only limits divine power to relate to finite persons as if God were a person (so Christians believe that God relates to us as Father in and through the person of the risen Christ). God also actively empowers finite persons, so as to give them a share in the divine reconciling and redeeming activity in the creation. In the moment of *henosis*, exemplified supremely in the person of Jesus, God enters into the being of those who freely consent to such mediating action and acts in and through them to make them living sacraments of the divine presence.

The third moment of the cosmic divine activity is *theosis*, that unity with or sharing in the divine life (2 Peter 1, 4) which is the final purpose of God for creation. As the Spirit unites with human nature to effect the divine purposes in creation, so human nature is ultimately raised to find its final destiny in sharing in the glory of God. The Christian tradition embodies the view that the whole of creation is in some way to be consummated in a 'new creation'. It is not merely to be relegated to a forgotten and transcended past. It is not to be continued in the same entropic way. It is to be taken into the eternal life of God and there transfigured into a new life. Paul describes that life as like wheat blossoming in the light of the sun, after its birth in the darkness of earth (I Corinthians 15). On that analogy, this cosmos is the soil in which the seeds of eternal life are sown. Its future will be unlike its present, and yet causally related to it – a consummation and not a cancellation of history.

It is extremely difficult for anyone to envisage such ultimate possibilities. But I think it is important to recover the truly cosmic sense of redemption that was characteristic both of the Biblical writings and of the Church Fathers. Redemption will not be seen as the saving of a few human beings from the destruction of one small planet. It will be seen as a reconstituting of the whole cosmos in the presence of God, in a more glorious form.[5] When Jesus proclaimed that the kingdom (the rule) of God was at hand, had come near (*engiken*), and was present and active in his own person, one way of understanding this is as an attempt to evoke a vision of each present moment as standing before the possibility of its own eternalisation in God. For any theist, it is true that God knows each present moment in the most intimate way. But as each finite moment is taken into the divine experience, it is transformed so that its negative qualities are mitigated and its positive qualities enhanced by the wider context of the divine experience. God's experience is of the world seen in the light of eternity, and so God knows things as no other being is able to know them.

Belief in *theosis* is belief that finite agents will be given a share in God's experience, so far as that is possible for them. They too will see temporal things in the light of eternity, and so see the events of history as having a purpose and pattern that is largely hidden *in via*. But this may still sound too much like a purely private and individual experience. It must be remembered that Christian belief is in the 'resurrection of the body'. It is not some form of disembodied experience of God. The forms of time and space themselves will be reiterated, but in a transformed way, free of decay and suffering. When the whole universe is so transformed that it manifests in an unrestricted way the beauty and goodness of God, and when personal beings, including human beings, are able to give conscious expression to this transformation, then the cosmos may indeed be said to share in the life of God.

For a Christian view, history is important. The resurrection world is not one that could just have been created perfect, without all the struggle and suffering that formed part of cosmic history.

---

[5] This is the vision of Pierre Teilhard de Chardin, whose life and thought is beautifully expounded by Ursula King in *Spirit of Fire* (Orbis, 2015).

The resurrection world is precisely a world formed out of struggle and conflict, a world perfected and not simply a world created perfect.

It may not be the case that the cosmos is already the body of God. It is perhaps too autonomous and its conscious agencies too self-willed for that. Yet its destiny is to be the body of God. For those who have lived and died with Christ will be raised in Christ (Colossians 2, 12). All things will be united in Christ (Ephesians 1, 10). Thus at that stage God will be all in all (1 Corinthians 15, 28), and there will no longer be a distinction between the Church and the world. There will be no Church and no separated world. The cosmos will be fully integrated into the life of God, as the vehicle of divine action and the manifestation of divine glory. In the moment of *theosis*, the cosmos is transfigured to become the unrestricted manifestation of God's glory, and all rational creatures become the instruments of his praise.

This is, quite properly in what is after all a theological work, put in terms of a fully Christian perspective. I think that Christian insights do deepen the sort of personal idealism which is one rational, coherent, and plausible possibility for philosophical thought. Even for those who are unable to accept a Christian view, one can show how a Christian view can be open, tolerant, and fully open to rational enquiry. The idea of a kenotic God who seeks to unite personal lives to the divine life is an idea that has intellectual and moral force. For Christians, it should show how philosophy can help broaden an understanding of faith and show that faith is not an irrational leap which is somehow opposed to reason.

There is a very definite cosmic vision implicit in a Christian view of creation as a kenotic and pleromal process. As the beginning of creation is *kenosis*, so the end or consummation of creation is *theosis*.

God shares in the pain and permits the wayward freedom of creatures in order that, finally, creatures should share in the bliss and become vehicles of the truly creative freedom of the divine nature. It is that cosmic movement from divine self-emptying to creaturely fulfilment in God which is the spiritual history of the cosmos, and, it seems to me, it is also the deepest meaning of the Christian Gospel for this planet in the middle of its journey through the mystery of time.

CHAPTER 21

Divine Causality

If mind is the ultimate cause and reality and the ultimate goal of all things, it will almost certainly play a positive role in the unfolding of the processes of the cosmos. When Aristotle thought about the causes of why things are the way they are, he decided that all things have what he called a 'final cause' – that for the sake of which they exist. Not only do things have an efficient cause, which is what brings them into being, but they also have a final cause, a reason for being the way they are or a goal at which they are aimed.

We might not today agree that everything has its own final cause, but if mind is the cause of the cosmos, then there will be a final cause of the cosmos as a whole. There will be that for the sake of which the cosmos exists, a purpose for which mind created the cosmos. We can think of that purpose as an idea in the mind of God which outlines what things are meant to be and what in the course of history they move towards being. Such an idea, because it exists in the mind of the being who brought the whole cosmos into being and because it gives the reason why the cosmos exists, will have some causal influence on the way the cosmos develops. There cannot be a purpose in the cosmos unless there exists some idea of the goal and some causal power to ensure that the goal is achieved. That idea exists in the mind of God, and God will ensure that the goal will be achieved.

I have suggested that God is not an all-determining sovereign. God creates a universe of autonomous, partly self-shaping persons and a universe which is open and emergent – not fully determined in every detail – and able to express itself in radically new creativity. That means that the goal, as it exists in the mind of God, is not fully determined either. It is no doubt determined in its general character – the goal will be to bring about a communion of free, intelligent, loving agents – but exactly what its nature will be is to be partly decided by the free acts of many creatures.

So we can think of God as cooperating with creatures in realising the goal of creation. God will guide and influence, but not wholly determine, the course of nature. Natural processes will have, as part of their causal structure, the ideals, existing in the mind of God, which attract things towards their actualisation.

We do not have much idea of the mechanics of this process. But then we have little idea of how ideas in human minds bring about changes in physical reality. It just seems that if we form an idea (say, of a house we want to build), that idea plays an important role in building the house, even though we know that there are lots of physical causes involved as well.

One way of thinking of this, which I explored in Part II, is to think of an idea as a piece of information, a sort of code for building physical elements, which is put into effect by lots of physical causes. The information plays a causal role, but it is not an efficient cause (part of the physical process which follows what we call 'laws of nature'). It is a sort of shaping cause, which could go wrong if the physical processes fail to incorporate the information.

So we could think of the ideal goal of free intelligent personhood, an idea in the mind of God. That information will shape the physical processes of the cosmos. But such shaping will be limited by the nature of those processes, which must allow for general causal laws, for chance or 'openness' in nature, and for the free choices of intelligent beings.[1]

At a sub-personal level, the ideals will inform and guide the direction of physical processes without those processes having any conscious awareness. But as finite minds emerge, they will become aware – to different degrees – of the ideals. They will then be able to either begin to realise them or possibly to frustrate them because of self-interest or rebelliousness. At the stage of full moral awareness, the ideals will then be seen either as attractive and desirable goals of action or as irksome and restrictive limitations on conduct. To put it another way, God will be seen as a desirable and attractive object of awareness or as a judgmental tyrant. It is not that God changes, but rather that God is seen differently according to human perspectives and choices of action.

The divine mind, like human minds, is not just a passive receptacle of ideals. It is an active causal power to realise these ideals. But as the divine mind interacts with finite minds, it will either act to enhance finite powers of realisation or act to frustrate them. There is an inspirational power to enable humans, for example, to rise to new heights of intuitive perception, courageous action, and creative endeavour. The divine powers of creativity, wisdom, and understanding cooperate with human minds, and these powers can be felt as a force outside and greater than oneself, yet working inwardly and in cooperation with oneself. The self becomes part of a greater whole with a greater power and purpose. Finite minds can participate in the mind of God, in its understanding and in its action, in ways which are possible and even natural for embodied and limited personal agents.

---

[1] A very fine outline of a closely similar view of God can be found in Thomas Jay Oord, *The Uncontrolling Love of God* (IVP Academic, 2015). In general, my view is close to that of the open and relational theology group of writers in the United States.

On the other hand, when these divine powers are taken away, finite minds are trapped in their own limiting perspectives, centred on self-interest, fear, and pride. Decay and destruction may not be immediate or inevitable in every case, but destruction is the natural consequence of separation from the one source of all power, creativity, and being. In this world, that division of participation in a wider creativity from self-destructiveness is not always clear. But in the world to come, when the personalities we have shaped have been decisively determined by what we have done in this world, the synergy or the separation of divine and human will become inescapably clear.

Divine causality is real. It does not consist in some supernatural person interfering to break unalterable laws of nature. It does not consist in God immediately punishing humans for evil actions and answering all the prayers of the righteous just as they are asked. Divine causality is the patient exercise of the power of the ideals for the sake of which the cosmos was created. The natural self-destructiveness of those who turn away from such ideals and such cooperative power, if it is not renounced, leads in the end to the elimination of those who have chosen the way of self-destruction. God will seek to heal and annul the power of self-destruction but will not compel finite minds to love the good and renounce evil – which compulsion would in fact be incompatible with any free assent to love. Thus divine causality is the patient attraction of love, the influence of which may be gentle and persuasive but which in the end is stronger than death.

This means that we do not have to pursue the difficult ideals of morality just by our own unaided efforts – a task in which most of us would probably fail. The power of divine creativity, sensitivity, understanding, cooperation, and compassion can strengthen our innermost selves so that they become capable of things beyond their normal reach. We might even want to say that to some extent it is God who lives and acts in and through us – though it would be wise to admit that the extent may be very small, as our friends would be quick to tell us. What we might call the Spirit of God places goodness within our hearts, with a power that is greater than ours and with an assurance that we will achieve the goal God desires for us, despite our own constant failures.

If we pray – that is, if we seek to conform our wills to a higher will and illuminate our minds by the wisdom of a greater mind – achieving the goal God desires for us should be the chief object of our prayer. We should ask that the power of God may live in our innermost selves and that it may enrich the lives of those whom we love and heal the lives of those to whom love seems impossible. We should ask that our self-love should be less, so that our love of goodness should increase, and that we should gradually become a channel for a love that is greater than our own, which nothing can finally defeat.

Suffering is often caused by the destructive behaviour of free agents. But the innocent suffer both because of the actions of others and because of natural diseases and disasters. Thus in our cosmos suffering is not proportioned to evildoing. Suffering is not properly thought of as a punishment for evil, though as a destructive force it often results from evil done by others or by oneself. Nor can suffering be thought of as a means to a greater good. It is not even plausible to think that all suffering can be used for some future good. Suffering is just bad, and it ought not to exist.

This needs some qualification, however. Some suffering results from the endeavour to overcome difficulties and problems. When that is plausible, such suffering can be accepted, though hardly enjoyed, as a necessary part of human existence. Some suffering results from a misuse of the freedom of others. Again, this can be accepted as part of existing in a world like this one, where freedom can be seen as the condition of potential fulfilment for everyone. Some suffering results from bad personal choices and must be accepted as a consequence of one's own imperfect actions. For all these sorts of suffering, being able to see that suffering as part of a wider whole which offers overwhelmingly greater good will enable one to accept and endure it. In the world to come, suffering of these sorts will fade and eventually cease, as one ascends to levels of being where the need for difficult striving and the occurrence of evil actions become less prevalent. We can often say that enduring such forms of suffering can help shape our characters as sympathetic, other-regarding, self-sacrificial moral agents. Insofar as we can see our sufferings as following from participation in a world which requires endurance, patience, and compassion from us, we can see suffering as part of our striving for virtue, even if such striving is forced upon us by circumstances we would never have chosen.

But not all suffering is like that. The suffering of young children most obviously cannot be seen as any sort of virtue formation. Nor can the suffering caused by natural disasters and by fatal diseases, which make any striving for virtue impossible. Even in these cases, a wider vision might be able to see how they are unpreventable parts of the only world in which we can come to exist as human beings. But that does not give our suffering any positive role to play in our formation. Nor can it be transformed into some future good. It is that sort of suffering which is simply bad and completely undesirable.

Perhaps all one can say is that in the world to come such suffering will cease. We will see then how our suffering has been necessary to the existence of a cosmos like ours and that it has come upon us not by specific design or intention, but rather as a result of general laws which operate without any reference to us in particular. It will always be part of our personal history, and it will therefore always be part of our unique experience. But its intensity and its debilitating influence will fade. When and only when that happens, we will begin to be able to use that past experience in a positive way, as it gives us greater understanding of the terrible and beautiful possibilities of being and enables us to share in a unique way in the mind of God, who knows all evils and who incorporates and transforms them within the infinite beatitude of the divine being.

If this is so, there will be many possibilities of growth and development in the world to come, as we reorder our earthly experiences in the light of growing knowledge of the wider reality of which this cosmos is only part. For most humans, many capacities and talents have been frustrated, misused, or neglected during life. It may be possible to find new ways of expressing and developing these capacities in the life to come.

Since there must be space for judgment, repentance, and purification in such a post-world existence, Christians might accept the many hints in the New Testament that there is a 'purification by fire'[2] and that a gradual growth is possible towards a final *apocatastasis*, the restoration of all things, as Gregory of Nyssa taught.[3]

At the end of our upper limit, as far as we can now conceive it, we will become wholly aware of the presence of God; have access to the contents of the mind of God; be filled with a deep love and regard for God; and fully cooperate with God in formulating, realising, and appreciating new forms of beauty and wisdom. Perhaps at that stage

[2] See, for instance, 1 Corinthians 3, 13–15: 'The work of each builder will become visible . . . the builder will be saved, but only as through fire.'

[3] The Greek term appears in Peter's sermon in Acts 3, 21, where he speaks of the 'restitution of all things'. A very good exposition of Gregory's thought is in Morwenna Ludlow's *Universal Salvation* (Oxford Monographs, 2009). Gregory speaks of the culmination of the process of purification as a 'passionless existence'. I would think that there would still be a place for affections and for change even after such a restoration, as a perfected human life might still be an infinite journey into God.

we will pass into forms of being we cannot now envisage. But those forms will be an expansion, not a loss, of the unique trajectories our lives have taken since their inception in this physical cosmos. We may even play a part in influencing for good the future of the physical cosmos, together with all those who achieve fulfilment in the life of God.

The thought of a final goal of the human journey, which is a full participation in the life of God and full communion with all others who complete that journey, can concentrate our minds on the deepest level of purpose in human existence. We are not accidents in a blind unconscious universe. We are agents who have a part to play in bringing the physical universe into union with God, in uniting the physical and spiritual in one sacramental unity. We will share in that unity, and we will then see the whole pattern of spiritual evolution into which all the many events of our lives fit. It does not have to be a goal predetermined in every detail. We may play our part by our thoughts and actions in deciding exactly what the details of that goal will be. But that the goal exists and will be realised, at least by all who join in pursuing it, is predetermined.

The classical, Aristotle-influenced idea of God is bound to believe in strong predestination, for God must create the whole of space-time in one non-temporal act. Therefore our future is predetermined by God's eternal decree, and God eternally knows what that which is future to us will be. But on an idealist view of God, the future is truly open and not wholly determined. Nevertheless, God has a goal in mind and is able to bring it about, though God may not unilaterally determine its exact form and nature.

God can thus be seen as having a definite purpose for the cosmos and for humanity, but not as determining in every detail what is to happen in human lives. Humans are free to sin and to accept or reject God's call. If so, God would not foreknow every detail of every human life. But God would foreknow that there would be intelligent and morally free finite persons. God intended from all eternity to call them, to justify, and to glorify them in Christ. The Greek word in the New Testament translated as 'predestined' is *pro-orisen*, and predestination need not have the specific technical meaning that it came to have in, for instance, Augustine and John Calvin. It can mean that God intended from the beginning that humans (all humans) should be called, justified, and glorified.[4] Yet if God does not compel humans to do what God wants, then in a sense God's intention can be frustrated (as, in fact, it is whenever humans sin). Whether that frustration will be final or only temporary we are hardly in a position to know. What we can know is that God wills the glorification of all and that God is able to bring it about if humans respond positively.

All we have to do is assent to the destiny that God wills, work towards it as best as we can, and put our faith in its ultimate realisation. And as we think of that far future, we may be able to make it present, albeit partially and imperfectly, in this physical world. The far future may be beyond time in its present form, in which the past is lost forever, the future is unknown, and the present is a transient moment that escapes our grasp even as we experience it. Time may come to have a different character, when in some way past, present, and future intertwine to make possible change without loss and anticipation without fear. To let that future break into every present time gives new meaning to human lives. Each moment becomes a sacrament of the completion of our temporal journey, and in those moments heaven lies around us, close enough to be seen and touched, though not yet to be grasped and held.

---

[4] The key passage is in Romans 8, 30: 'Those whom [God] predestined he also called; and those whom he called he also justified; and those whom he justified he also glorified.'

CHAPTER 22

Reason and Revelation

I have been exploring the implications of positing the priority of mind in the universe, given the observed nature of our cosmos. I have argued that this postulate is reasonable and plausible, and in fact I think that it is the most adequate available philosophical description of the nature of reality. But a postulate can seem like an abstract intellectual exercise. To counter this feeling, I have tried to draw some practical implications about care for the natural world, empathy with other human beings, the importance of pursuing moral values for their own sake, and the existence of life-changing and transformative experiences which form the heart of belief in God for millions of people.

Few people engage in philosophical speculation. But millions of people have a vivid belief in God, in a personal reality at the very centre of their experience of the world. I think that philosophy gives invaluable help in coping with some of the problems of religious belief, once someone comes across those problems. But philosophy is rarely the motivating force of belief in God.

That motivating force is experience. It is an experience of the personal presence of the cosmic mind that underlies the universe, an experience that comes as a revelation of the otherwise hidden nature of reality. Just as scientific theories, however beautiful and elegant, need to be confirmed by some experience, often of a highly technical and rather rare sort, so philosophical postulates are enriched if they can be confirmed by experience, even if those experiences in their fullness are rare and open only to especially wise and sensitive individuals.

Such experiences of ultimate mind may take many different forms, and often they may not even be identified as experiences of mind. Human minds are expressed in works of art, music, and poetry, but those works can be just valued for themselves, without thinking about their creators. So the mind of God will be expressed through the wonders of the natural world. It will be expressed in the human striving for ideals of beauty and of goodness. Those ideals may be valued, and rightly, for themselves, but I believe that they are given a greater objective reality and normative force by being located as objective possibilities in the mind of God.

In the appreciation of the integrated complexity of the physical world, in the inspirations which take human minds beyond their normal capacities, and in the sense of a transcendent presence of value and significance which can occur at crucial moments of human experience, we may properly speak of encounter with the mind of God.

As the human body expresses the human mind, so the world in which we live expresses the divine mind, and we can appreciate such expressions without explicitly believing in the existence of some supernatural being. Yet as some movements and actions of the human body express our minds more fully and clearly than others, so some events and occurrences in the world of our experience express the mind of God more fully and clearly. And as some people are more than usually open and sensitive to the minds of others, so we might expect that some people are more open and sensitive to the mind of the cosmos than most of us are.

If there is a God, some experiences will be more truly disclosive of God's reality than others, and it is natural to expect that God will actively seek to reveal the divine nature in some way. This active seeking results in what is called 'revelation' – a disclosure of the presence of God in some vivid experience, which may or may not include words.[1]

Christianity claims that in the person of Jesus there was a critical point in history when the human apprehension of God and the divine act of self-disclosure came together in a unique and decisive way. Obviously such a claim could not be established simply by some philosophical theory about the nature of the reality. It rests on the historical fact that Jesus' human mind had uniquely intimate awareness of God and that the divine mind was actively expressed in him in a unique way.

Many philosophical views that posit a God think of that God as so different and distant from finite human beings that there is no way in which they could be united. God is virtually unlimited in power and knowledge, and is incapable of making silly or self-centred choices. Humans are weak and ignorant, and are always making silly and egoistic choices. How could the creative source of a billion galaxies have anything to do with a race of two-legged puny animals hopping about on the surface of one tiny planet?

But maybe belief in such a remote God underestimates the power of God. A God who was supremely powerful would not be condemned to be remote and distant from creatures. It would show more power if God could also be in intimate relationship with millions of creatures. Though the power of God would sustain the galaxies, it could also have intimate knowledge of the inner lives of sentient beings on one tiny planet like the earth. Christianity claims that God takes one brief human life, the life of Jesus, and unites it to the divine nature itself. In doing so, God shows that God

[1] I have given a fuller account of the nature of revelation in 'Religion and Revelation' (Oxford University Press, 1994).

is concerned for the lives of individual human and sentient beings. God wills their good and well-being. God acts in particular and personal ways to develop their knowledge and love of the divine. And God does so by the very particular act of taking one human life and making it the definitive vehicle of God's own loving action and the revelation of God's nature and purpose.

Revelation, for Christians, is a self-unveiling of the personal being of God, and it comes in and through a personal life. Jesus did not write a book, and what has been preserved and treasured are not any exact words that he wrote, but the impact he made on those who followed him. Christians will naturally think that the Gospels and other writings in the New Testament are authentic records of that impact – that even if we do not have Jesus' exact words (which were probably in Aramaic) we have treasured memories of his teachings and records of the major events of his life and actions. So the Bible is of immense importance, and we may well wish to say that its accounts have been inspired by God so that they do convey to us the true nature of Jesus' person and life. But the fact remains that it is encounter with the person of Jesus, possible above all in the community of the Church and through the action of the Holy Spirit, which is the central point of Christian revelation.

The New Testament writings are based on experience, the unique experience of Jesus himself (though that is not directly available to us) and the experience the devotees and disciples of Jesus had when they met the Lord (some of which was later remembered and recorded in the New Testament Gospels). St. Paul became a disciple after a visionary experience. The first disciples were inspired by the experience of the Spirit descending upon them at Pentecost. Experience is central to Christian revelation and faith.

It is in the Biblical tradition that the idea of God as a personal moral will gradually take shape, until (for Christians) it reaches a culminating point in a person who by his life and teaching deepens the demands of morality so that they speak of self-giving love for all people without exception and who by his death and resurrection reveals the purpose of God to fulfil and transform the created cosmos.

The philosophy of personal idealism thus finds a particular historical expression in Jesus Christ, who unequivocally reveals God as a personal Creator of self-sacrificial love with a moral purpose for creation.

As with most human knowledge, this revelation comes at a specific time and to a specific people. But the rest of humanity is not excluded from knowledge of God. According to the idealist view I have outlined, divine action is mainly a matter of influencing and gradually deepening human perceptions and thoughts. It is not a matter of simply ignoring them or replacing them with miraculous divine knowledge. So we might expect that there would be a number of different philosophical and evaluative viewpoints among early humans and that they would develop in differing ways in different cultures and histories. Christians can see a definite and important influence of God in religious views that see ultimate reality as a way of harmony with nature (the *Tao*), as an impersonal 'pure mind', as an all-including Absolute reality, or as a sovereign Lord who does not enter into creation to share its sufferings and experiences. Many of the world's religions are able to relate to the one reality which can lead them from egoism to what John Hick calls 'reality-centredness'.[2] But if God really is a personal self-sacrificing creator, and if personal idealism is true, then it is in the tradition of the God of Abraham, the Biblical God, that God is revealed most adequately.

---

[2] I have written about how many of the world's religions converge on the idea of a spiritual centre in *Concepts of God* (Oneworld Press, 1998).

Of course there is not just one unchanging idea of 'the Biblical God'. Like all human ideas, there have been developments of thought as divine revelation has cooperated with initial human values and concepts to come to a clearer idea of the God of Abraham. Christians can see the Old Testament as a gradual development of perceptions about the true nature of God. At first God was just one among many gods. But in Isaiah it is seen that there is only one true God. At first God held whole families guilty for the crime of one man, but Ezekiel comes to see that a person should be held guilty only of their own crimes. At first the Bible taught that there is a law of strict revenge – an eye for an eye and a tooth for a tooth. But Jesus taught that we should not oppose evil, and that instead we should turn the other cheek.

So it seems reasonable to believe that perceptions of God's nature and purpose developed throughout the many centuries over which the Bible was composed and edited. It is a record of the developing perceptions of those who were devoted to God and inspired by God. It follows that divine revelation takes humans where they are and influences, but does not wholly determine, their beliefs so that their perceptions of God become more accurate. Christians think that in Jesus the apprehension of God achieved a new and definitive form. For in Jesus the self-giving love of God was expressed in an astonishing way.

Even so, while the New Testament records the impact Jesus made on his disciples, that impact has often been inadequately perceived in many cases. It took over a thousand years for slavery to be seen as in conflict with the belief that all humans are the children of God and are to be respected as such. Even today there are some people who cannot see that treating women as subservient to men is just as much in conflict with divine revelation. What they need to see and acknowledge is that no humans see divine revelation in its fullness.

And that goes for those who have seen divine revelation in Jesus as well as those who lived before Jesus and did not have the benefit of his presence or teaching.

We might hope, however, that experiences of God might serve to deepen our moral insights and teach us that a God of universal love and concern is more truly good than a God of vengeance and rigid adherence to unchangeable laws. The teaching of Jesus – that God is a God of mercy and forgiveness and that what matters in human life is the cultivation of a universally inclusive love – seems fairly clear about this.

As well as developments in moral sensibility, there have been major developments in our understanding of the universe which affect the ways in which we think about God. Here again, experiences of God must be consistent with the best available knowledge of the nature of reality, with the proviso that even the best available knowledge may turn out to be inadequate in many ways. Because of this we should never claim that we know certainly and absolutely what God is like. What we can and must do is continue to make our beliefs about God consistent with the best moral and factual beliefs that we possess. This will not resolve all disagreements, but it will help us acknowledge that the attempt to achieve a morally and factually adequate view of God is a difficult and developing process. In this respect, beliefs about God are not very different from beliefs about morality or about the nature of the physical universe. We must live by the most adequate view of which we are aware and take care to be sure that we are aware of the widest and most relevant new knowledge that is available to us.

Some ideas of God have been influenced, and in many cases hampered, by very inadequate moral and factual beliefs. It is rather unlikely that we now have a wholly adequate idea of God, but at least we can see that the purposes of a creative mind of a vast cosmos like ours are unlikely to be limited to the very short history of human beings on one small blue planet. There is much yet to be done to develop our understanding of the nature of God as it was revealed in Jesus Christ. So the form of Christian belief that seems most appropriate to the human situation is one which is open and expansive: it is open to change and expansion in the light of new moral and factual knowledge and insights from other views of life, and it is inclusive of all humanity, not limited to a concern with the salvation of just one small group of believers.[3] But it can still be committed to loyalty to the person and teaching of Jesus Christ as the decisive revelation on earth of the nature, person, and presence of God and the historical focus of God's action to redeem the world from evil.

I have outlined a philosophy of personal idealism as a reasonable and convincing account of the nature of reality in the context of modern morality and science. I think that this philosophy is certainly consistent with the central Christian view that there exists a personal God whose nature is self-giving love and whose purpose is that all created intelligences should find fulfilment in a community of love. This specifically Christian view is not founded just on philosophical speculation but also on the impact made on his disciples by the life, death, and resurrection appearances of Jesus. It is based on revelation, and what I have wanted to say in this final chapter is that, while an analysis of revelation is not the topic of this

---

[3] John Hick, in *An Interpretation of Religion* (Macmillan, 1989), provides what has become a standard classification of religious attitudes into exclusivist and pluralist, to which his pupil Alan Race added a third possibility – that of inclusivism. Exclusive views claim to have the only truth and to offer the only path to salvation. Inclusive views claim to have the truth but allow that other faiths can have parts of the truth and may be less direct ways to salvation. Pluralist views claim that many religions are more or less equally true and are equally good paths to salvation. Hick himself is a pluralist and believes that the ultimately 'Real' is unknown and beyond all human descriptions. I do not think that the Real is beyond all description, and I do think that some traditions give more adequate descriptions than others. But no tradition is likely to possess all the truth, so I would prefer to recommend that each tradition should seek to be both self-critical and open to learn from what others have to teach. Perhaps this could be called a fourth, 'expansivist' view. Traditions should seek to be 'inclusive' with regard to salvation, in excluding no one from salvation (or final fulfilment), but they should not claim to be either the sole bearers of truth or to be inclusive of all religious truths.

book, it is natural to think that if there is the God that personal idealists think there is, we would expect that it would reveal its nature and purpose in some way. Revelation cannot be reduced to philosophical reason, but certain sorts of philosophical reason lead one to be open to some historical self-disclosure of the ultimate source of all beings.

It is of course possible to be a personal idealist without being a Christian – indeed without belonging to any religious tradition – and it is possible to be a Christian without being a personal idealist. But I think there is a natural affinity between Christianity and personal idealism. Christians understand the supreme mind as a God of self-giving and redemptive love, and they aim, at their best, to live in the way of the Spirit of Christ, a way which can mediate that love to the world. It seems to me that personal idealism provides a sound rational and reflective basis for such a faith and that Christian faith provides a form of life that gives appropriate practical expression to the speculations of personal idealist philosophy. Here, at least, reason and faith embrace and enfold each other.

Bibliography

Note: I have not cited specific editions of classical philosophical texts except where I have quoted from them.

Anselm, *Proslogion* (1078)

Aquinas, Thomas, *The Light of Faith* (Sophia Press, 1993)
    Summa Theologiae (ed. T. Gilby et al.; Blackfriars, 1964–1981)

Aristotle, *De Anima*

Aristotle, *Metaphysics*
    Nicomachean Ethics

Athanasius, *On the Incarnation* (*De Incarnatione*, trans. R. W. Thomason; Clarendon Press, 1971)

Augustine, *De Trinitate* (trans. Edmund Hill, New City Press, 1991)

Ayer, A. J., *The Central Questions of Philosophy* (Weidenfeld and Nicolson, 1973)
    Language, Truth and Logic (Victor Gollancz, 1936)

Barrett, Justin L., *Cognitive Science, Religion, and Theology* (Templeton Press, 2011)

Barth, Karl, *Church Dogmatics*, vol. 2 (ed. G. W. Bromiley and T. F. Torrance, T and T Clark, 1937)

Berkeley, George, *Three Dialogues between Hylas and Philonous* (1713)

Bradley, F. H., *Ethical Studies* (Clarendon Press, 1927)

Buber, Martin, *I and Thou* (trans. Ronald Gregor Smith, T and T Clark, 1958; first published 1923)

Camus, Albert, *The Plague (La Peste)* (English edition, Hamish Hamilton, 1947)

Cartwright, Nancy, *The Dappled World* (Cambridge University Press, 1999)

Cartwright, Nancy and Ward, Keith, *Re-Thinking Order* (Bloomsbury, 2016)

Conway Morris, Simon, *Life's Solution* (Cambridge University Press, 2003)

Cottingham, John, *Cartesian Reflections* (Oxford University Press, 2008)
Why Believe? (Continuum, 2009)

Crick, Francis, *The Astonishing Hypothesis* (Simon and Schuster, 1994)

Darwin, Charles, *The Origin of Species* (1859)

Davies, Paul, *The Mind of God* (Simon and Schuster, 1992)

Davies, Paul and Gregersen, Niels, *Information and the Nature of Reality* (Cambridge University Press, 2010)

Davies, Paul and Gribbin, John, *The Matter Myth* (Penguin, 1992)

Dawkins, Richard, *The God Delusion* (Bantam, 2006)

Dennett, Daniel, *Consciousness Explained* (Penguin, 1991)

D'Espagnat, Bernard, *Reality and the Physicist* (Cambridge University Press, 1990)

Einstein, Albert, *Festschrift for Aunel Stadola* (Orell Fussli, 1929)

Ellis, Fiona, *God, Values, and Nature* (Oxford University Press, 2014)

Fiddes, Paul, *The Creative Suffering of God* (Clarendon, 1988)
Past Event and Present Salvation (Darton, Longman, Todd, 1989)

Foster, John, *The Case for Idealism* (Routledge, 1982)
The Immaterial Self (Routledge, 1991)

Gottlieb, Roger (ed.), *This Sacred Earth* (Routledge, 1966)

Gould, Stephen J., 'Non-Moral Nature', in *The Sacred Beetle* (ed. M. Gardner, Oxford University Press, 1985)

Gregory of Nyssa, 'On the Soul and Resurrection', in *The Nicene and Post-Nicene Fathers*, vol. 5 (trans. A. H. Wilson, T and T Clark, 1988)

Hawking, Stephen, *A Brief History of Time* (Bantam, 1988)

Hawking, Stephen and Mlodinow, Leonard, *The Grand Design* (Bantam, 2011)

Hegel, Georg Wilhelm Friedrich, *Phenomenology of Spirit* (1807), trans. A. V. Miller (Oxford University Press, 1977)
The Science of Logic (1812–1818, trans. George di Giovanni, Oxford University Press, 2010)

Hick, John, *Death and Eternal Life* (Macmillan, 1976)
An Interpretation of Religion (Macmillan, 1989)

Hume, David, *An Enquiry concerning the Principles of Morals* (1751)
A Treatise of Human Nature (1739)

Huxley, T. H., *Evolution and Ethics* (Pilot Press, 1947)

Jackson, Frank, 'What Mary Didn't Know', *Journal of Philosophy* 83, no. 5 (1986)

Jammer, M., *The Philosophy of Quantum Theory* (Wiley, 1974)

Kant, Immanuel, *The Critique of Pure Reason* (1781)

    Lectures on Ethics (1782, trans. Louis Infield, Harper, 1963)

    Prolegomena (1783)

    Religion within the Limits of Reason Alone (1794)

Kierkegaard, Søren, *Concluding Unscientific Postscript* (1846, trans. Alastair Hannay, Cambridge University Press, 2009)

King, Ursula, *Spirit of Fire* (Orbis, 2015)

Leibniz, *Monadology* (1714)

Leslie, John, *Universes* (Routledge, 1994)

Libet, Benjamin, 'Do We Have Free Will?' in *The Volitional Brain* (ed. Libet, Freeman, and Sutherland, Imprint Academic, 1999)

Ludlow, Morwenna, *Universal Salvation* (Oxford Monographs, 2009)

Mawson, T. J., *Free Will: A Guide for the Perplexed* (Continuum, 2001)

McGinn, Colin, *The Problem of Consciousness* (Basil Blackwell, 1991)

Meister, Chad (ed.), 'The Doctrine of the Trinity', *Philosophia Christi* 17, no. 3 (November, 2016)

Mill, John Stuart, *Utilitarianism* (1861)

Murdoch, Iris, *The Sovereignty of Good* (Routledge, 1970)

Nadeau, Robert and Kafatos, Menas, *The Non-Local Universe* (Oxford University Press, 1999)

Nagel, Thomas, 'What Is It Like to Be a Bat?' *Philosophical Review* 83, no. 4 (1974)

Oord, Thomas Jay, *The Uncontrolling Love of God* (IVP Academic, 2015)

Otto, Rudolf, *The Idea of the Holy* (1917, English translation, Oxford University Press, 1923)

Page, Ruth, *God and the Web of Creation* (SCM Press, 1996)

Peacocke, Arthur, *Creation and the World of Science* (Clarendon, 1979)

    Paths from Science towards God (Oneworld Press, 2001)

Penrose, Roger, *Shadows of the Mind* (Oxford University Press, 1994)

Plantinga, Alvin, *The Nature of Necessity* (Oxford University Press, 1974)

    Where the Conflict Really Lies (Oxford University Press, 2011)

Plato, *The Republic*

    Timaeus

Polkinghorne, John, *Exploring Reality* (Yale University Press, 2005)

Ramachandran, V. S., *The Tell-Tale Brain* (Windmill, 2012)

Ramanuja, *The Vedanta Sutras* (trans. George Thibaut, in Sacred Books of the East, vol. 48, Motilal Banarsidass, 1962)

Ruse, Michael, *Evolutionary Naturalism* (Routledge, 1995)

Ryle, Gilbert, *The Concept of Mind* (Hutchinson, 1949)

Sartre, Jean-Paul, *Huis Clos* (1944)

Schleiermacher, Friedrich, *On Religion: Speeches to Its Cultured Despisers* (1799, trans. Richard Crouter, Cambridge University Press, 1988)

Searle, John, 'Minds, Brains, and Programs', *Behavioural and Brain Sciences* 3 (1980)

The Rediscovery of the Mind (MIT Press, 1992)

Strawson, Peter, *Individuals* (Methuen, 1959)

Swinburne, Richard, *The Coherence of Theism* (Oxford University Press, 1977)

The Evolution of the Soul (Oxford University Press, 1986)

Mind, Brain and Free Will (Oxford University Press, 2013)

Teilhard de Chardin, Pierre, *The Phenomenon of Man* (Collins, 1959, re-issued as *The Human Phenomenon*)

Tipler, Frank J., *The Physics of Immortality* (Doubleday, 1994)

Ward, Keith, *The Big Questions in Science and Religion* (Templeton Press, 2008)

Christ and the Cosmos (Cambridge University Press, 2016)

Concepts of God (Oneworld Press, 1998)

'Cosmos and Kenosis', in *The Work of Love* (ed. John Polkinghorne, SPCK, 2001)

'Freedom, Necessity and Suffering in God', in *Within the Love of God* (ed. Anthony Clarke and Andrew Moore, Oxford University Press, 2014)

'Idealism and the Moral Life', in *Idealism and Christian Philosophy* (ed. Steven Cowan and James Spiegel, Bloomsbury Academic, 2016)

Morality, Autonomy, and God (Oxford, Oneworld Press, 2013)

More Than Matter (Lion Hudson, 2010)

Rational Theology and the Creativity of God (Blackwell, 1982)

Religion and Revelation (Oxford University Press, 1994)

Weinberg, Steven, *The First Three Minutes* (Andre Deutsch, 1977)

Wheeler, John, 'The Past and the Delayed-Choice Double-Slit Experiment', in *Mathematical Foundations of Quantum Theory* (ed. A. R. Marlow, Academic Press, 1978)

White, Lynn, 'The Historical Roots of Our Ecological Crisis', *Science* 155
   (1967)
Whitehead, A. N. *Process and Reality* (Macmillan, 1929)
Wigner, Eugene, 'The Unreasonable Effectiveness of Mathematics in
   Natural Sciences', *Communications in Pure and Applied Mathematics*
   13, no. 1 (1960)
Wittgenstein, Ludwig, *Philosophical Investigations* (ed. G.E.M. Anscombe,
   Blackwell, 1974)

Index

Of main themes and terms, and persons who are quoted or discussed in the text